St. Augustine

Rodney and Loretta Carlisle

Jacksonville Fl
Books million
12-16-18
SUN.

Pineapple Press, Inc.
Sarasota, Florida

Inquiries should be addressed to:
Pineapple Press, Inc.
P.O. Box 3889
Sarasota, Florida 34230

www.pineapplepress.com

Library of Congress Cataloging-in-Publication Data

Carlisle, Rodney P.
    St. Augustine in history / Rodney and Loretta Carlisle. – First Edition.
    pages   cm
Includes index.
ISBN 978-1-56164-681-4 (pbk. : alk. paper)
1. Saint Augustine (Fla.) – History. I. Carlisle, Loretta. II. Title. III. Title: Saint Augustine in history.
    F319.S2C37 2014
    975.9'18—dc23

2013038978

First Edition
10 9 8 7 6 5 4 3 2 1

All photographs are by Loretta Carlisle unless otherwise noted.
Design by Shé Hicks
Printed in the United States

Contents

Introduction

St. Augustine, Florida, is itself a physical documentation of the past. The ancient homes, forts, cemeteries, and streets of the city tell a rich story. That story goes back to the first sighting of Florida in 1513 and to the city's founding by the Spanish in 1565, long before Jamestown and Plymouth Rock. Archaeological sites in St. Augustine tell us more about that history and about the Native American people who lived in the area and throughout Florida for thousands of years before the first Europeans arrived.

The purpose of this book is to provide a summary of the findings of historians and archaeologists that put the rich collection of sites and artifacts in St. Augustine in context. Each chapter is devoted to a period of that long history and includes the findings of specialists, as well as descriptions and photographs of the places where you can see the past.

For local historians, nearby history provides other kinds of documentation besides the papers in archives and volumes in libraries. The design, style, and layout of ancient houses are themselves physical documents, showing how builders and residents saw daily life in the past. Fragments of lost items, such as broken pottery, coins, jewelry, and household items, give clues to exactly when residents lost them and how affluent they were. A cemetery is rich in documents—not only on the gravestones, with their testimony to the lifespan of individuals and families, but in the variety of surnames, reflecting the ethnic origins of prior generations. Structural details such as building materials, doors, windows, and floor plans give links to time and place. Fortifications, government buildings, and the very layout of streets all tell their tales. Artifacts preserved and on display in museums, such as tools, utensils, costumes, weapons, and furniture, all document small but important aspects of daily life.

The history documented in this way in St. Augustine may offer some surprises. St. Augustine is the oldest city in the continental United States continuously inhabited by people of European descent. It was also at the center of severe wars between England and Spain for control of North America over a period of 250 years. The city saw real pirates storm ashore and street-by-street exchanges of musket fire and sword fights between raiders and defenders. It was the destination for escaped slaves who established their own "underground railroad" that ran south to the sanctuaries offered by the Spanish and by Native Americans.

When the United States acquired Florida in 1821, St. Augustine almost immediately became a destination for visitors escaping the harsh winters of the North. The city played crucial roles in the Second Seminole War and the American Civil War. Refugees who sought sanctuary within the city during both of those conflicts shaped the city's history. By the end of the Civil War, the ethnic mix included not only descendants of the Spanish and English Colonial Periods, including Greeks, Italians, and Minorcans, but a large African-American presence as well.

In more modern times, St. Augustine was at the center of transportation revolutions, both railroad and automotive, that reshaped how Americans traveled and how tourism itself became a commercial enterprise. It became a destination for wealthy vacationers, a "winter Newport" that rivaled the elite summer vacation spot of the very wealthy in Rhode Island. Like other cities in the South, during World War II the city saw an influx of thousands of draftees and volunteers, stationed at nearby training camps or directly in the city. Partly because of the city's fame as a travel destination and partly because of its rich multi-ethnic heritage, it was at the center of the Civil Rights reforms of the 1960s.

The book is presented in seven chapters by chronological era. Each presents the history of a period as it affected St. Augustine and

Florida to establish the context of the era, and each chapter concludes with a section describing present-day facilities and attractions that relate to the period. These are the seven periods:

Pre-Colonial and "Discovery": to 1565
First Spanish Period: 1565–1763
British Period: 1763–1783
Second Spanish Period: 1784–1821
Territorial and Early Statehood: 1821–1861
Civil War and Gilded Age: 1861–1913
World War I to the Present: 1914–2013

Documentation for the information in this book was drawn from many sources, including not only books, published articles, and Internet sources but also the many historical markers and brochures available at the sites visited as well. A list of sources, arranged by chapter, is provided at the end of the book.

For the visitor, the sites themselves are the physical documents that back up the story. The whole focus of this work is what you can see that tells the story of each period. No other city in the continental United States has sites that reflect five centuries of history. This short guide can help you unravel that story.

Chapter 1
THE FOUNDING OF ST. AUGUSTINE
1513–1565

Ponce de León

From 1513 to 1565, the Spanish launched many separate expeditions that touched on Florida, but that of Juan Ponce de León became a source of legend.

In 1512 the king of Spain granted Ponce a charter to explore for new land. He sailed west with two ships, a pilot by the name

This life-size statue of Ponce de León is striking. Ponce was just under five feet tall.

of Antón de Alaminos, and two native captives who knew the East Coast of North America and served as guides. On April 2, 1513, they spotted land and sailed along the coastal barrier islands, seeking a harbor. One calculation puts their landing about fifty miles south of St. Augustine at the present-day Ponce Inlet. Ponce went ashore on Sunday, April 3. Seeing the abundant wildflowers and aware that it was the Easter season, Ponce named what he thought was an island after the "flowery Passover," *Pascua Florida.*

After leading several other expeditions, Ponce returned to Florida, sailing on February 15, 1521, from San Juan, Puerto Rico, to Sanibel Island on the west coast of Florida. In an encounter with the natives, they wounded him with an arrow. The injury did not heal, and he sailed for Havana in search of medical treatment, where he died in July 1521. His body now rests in the Cathedral in San Juan, Puerto Rico, where his crypt can be visited to this day.

Ponce de León

Some details of Ponce de Leon's life have never been established with certainty. We know that he was born between 1460 and 1470 in Leon, Spain, and died in 1521 in Havana, Cuba. There is evidence he was a member of Columbus's second expedition in 1493. By 1502 he was on Hispaniola, the island shared today by the Dominican Republic and Haiti.

Ponce de León was the first governor of Puerto Rico from 1509 to 1511. He led an exploration of the Bahamas, landing in Florida, probably near Melbourne Beach, on April 2, 1513. It was the Easter season, so Ponce named the land *La Florida* for *Pascua Florida,* which means "Flowery Passover," or Easter. The name was appropriate for a magical, flowery territory.

The legend arose that he was in search of a fabled Fountain of Youth. In fact, he was probably looking for gold. In 1514 he returned to Spain and was appointed military governor of Cuba. He led an unsuccessful expedition to colonize Florida in 1521, when he was wounded in a battle with Native Americans. He returned to Cuba and died the same year.

The Legend of Ponce de León's Fountain

A fountain-of-youth legend claimed that Ponce arrived in Florida searching for a well or fountain with water that could rejuvenate elderly people. The legend grew and the search for youth became a lasting symbol of the European conquest and settlement of the New World.

1565: The Threat from the French

The French plan that spurred the Spanish to make a permanent settlement at St. Augustine sprang from the religious conflicts of the era. Catherine Di Medici, regent for the young French monarch Charles IX, sponsored the resettlement of members of a Protestant religious sect called the Huguenots from France to Florida in the 1560s. She sought to remove them from persecution in France—and she saw the settlement as a way to extend French power in the New World.

In 1565 King Philip II of Spain learned of the group of Huguenots in Florida at Fort Caroline near present-day Jacksonville. From the Spanish Catholic viewpoint, not only did the French invade Spanish territory, they planned to settle Spanish lands with heretics. Philip sent Pedro Menéndez de Avilés as *adelantado de mar*—expedition military commander, or "admiral"—with the charge to stop the French. He ordered Menéndez to find and completely destroy the French settlement at Fort Caroline, sparing only Catholics.

Menéndez exchanged some gunshots with the French at Fort Caroline and then sailed south, where, on September 8, he landed at Seloy village. The landing spot was almost certainly at the open space in front of the present-day Mission Nombre de Dios. St. Augustine traces its founding to this 1565 landing, just north of the center of town.

On landing, the fleet chaplain, Father Lopez Mendoza Grajales, held a Catholic Mass. Menéndez named the site after the feast day of St. Augustine of Hippo, August 28, the day when he had first sighted Florida.

Augustine the Saint

Saint Augustine (354–430) was the Catholic bishop of Hippo Regius (present-day Annaba, Algeria). After converting to Christianity at age thirty-three, Augustine developed his own writings on philosophy and theology. His work on just and unjust wars is still pertinent today. He developed the idea of a City of God that was distinct from the earthly states ruled by kings and emperors. Through the Medieval period, the City of God included all worshippers in the Catholic faith under the jurisdiction of the Church. Saint Augustine not only inspired Menéndez to name his settlement in Florida; he is also the patron saint of theologians, printers, and beer brewers.

The local Timucua people watched the Mass, impressed by the ceremony. A mural in the Cathedral facing the town square depicts the scene. The chief of Seloy welcomed Menéndez and his troops, offering them the long house in which to stay. The Spanish immediately began fortifying the structure by digging a surrounding ditch and installing a stockade.

The First Thanksgiving

Dr. Michael Gannon, a leading Florida historian and expert, has pointed out that the first Thanksgiving in a permanent European settlement in North America was celebrated in Florida on September 8, 1565, not in November 1621 at Plymouth, Massachusetts. Under the leadership of Father Lopez, a Mass of Thanksgiving was performed for the safe arrival of the Spanish settlers. After the Mass, Menéndez laid out a feast and invited the native people of Seloy to attend. September 8 is the feast day of the Nativity of the Blessed Virgin Mary in the Catholic calendar.

Menéndez at Seloy

Archaeologists are still trying to locate the exact spot in the village of Seloy where Menéndez took over the large council house. Unfortunately, the exact size and shape of the building are unknown. Some historical documents suggest the structure would have been large, perhaps big enough to hold a village assembly. We do know that after Menéndez occupied the building and built a moat around it, he stored munitions in it; some of the colonists probably lived in the structure during the winter of 1565–66.

Menéndez and his eight hundred Spaniards soon wore out their welcome with the Seloy villagers. The native people burned part of the fortified council house and drove the Spanish off in the spring of 1566. Menendez resettled on Anastasia Island, building another encampment with a wooden fort there. Then in the 1570s, he moved again, to the present site of the city of St. Augustine.

The Massacres

At Fort Caroline, the French heard reports of the Spanish settlement at Seloy and decided on an immediate attack by sea. Some five hundred Frenchmen in five ships sailed south on September 11, 1565. The force outnumbered the Spanish under Menéndez, but the attack by sea was a bad choice.

Foul winds drove the French ships far to the south, where they wrecked. The straggling survivors landed on beaches in at least two separate parties, probably between present-day Daytona Beach and Cape Canaveral, more than fifty miles south of St. Augustine. They began a march along the coast northward, encountering a waterway break in the shoreline at Matanzas Inlet and stopping there.

Meanwhile, Menéndez first led a force that seized Fort Caroline, killing 130 soldiers and civilians. He captured a few surviving women and children. Menéndez then led about seventy well-armed Spanish troops south to stop the shipwrecked French forces. Finding one party stalled at the inlet, he demanded their surrender. Exhausted, without weapons, and weakened from thirst and hunger, the French had no choice and gave up. Nearly all declared themselves Protestants.

Menéndez ordered the Spanish troops to slaughter the French soldiers with swords and knives. He did not want to waste gunpowder on the defenseless captives. At the inlet, Menéndez reputedly spared sixteen Frenchmen who professed to be Catholic. On October 11, 1565, the Spanish stopped a second group of French soldiers at the same inlet and again executed most of them. A few French from the second party escaped on foot; the Spanish tracked them down somewhere near Cape Canaveral and sent them off to Havana as

This portrait of Pedro Menéndez de Aviles, the founder of St. Augustine, is located in the Spring House at the Fountain of Youth Park.

prisoners along with the women and children from Fort Caroline.

Two slaughters occurred at the inlet, hence the name *matanzas,* the Spanish plural for "massacre." Although the exact spots of the killings have never been located, Fort Matanzas was later built at the mouth of the inlet, and the waterway between Anastasia Island and St. Augustine is named Matanzas River.

SITES TO SEE

Fountain of Youth Archaeological Park

A commercial venture since the early 1900s, the Fountain of Youth Archaeological Park encourages you to identify with many of the historical and legendary aspects of the first Europeans' contact with

The Fountain of Youth Park has been welcoming visitors since the early 1900s.

Native Americans at the spot. A map shows the major archaeological finds on the grounds and the location of several attractions. Historical tourism has evolved from fanciful and outlandish claims and sensational presentations to well-documented, educational sites. You can get a glimpse of the "history of historical presentation," or history through "attractions," as you look at some of the ways material is presented at the site.

At the Spring House, costumed interpreters provide an account of Ponce de León's exploration. They also relate the more modern story of the purchase of the property by Dr. Luella Day McConnell around 1900. They explain the discovery of artifacts on the site, such as a silver saltshaker from the early Spanish settlement. The park guides formerly claimed that Ponce himself had placed the stone cross embedded in the ground near the spring. Its fifteen vertical stones and thirteen in the cross bar denoted the year 1513. It was a nice story, but in the interest of historical accuracy, it is no longer told.

The Discovery Globe, a two-story structure installed in

This life-size diorama display at the Fountain of Youth Park Spring House represents a first encounter between Spanish explorers and native Timucua people.

Luella Day McConnell presented this artesian well as the original Fountain of Youth sought by Ponce de León. There is no charge for a drink of water.

1959, shows the exploration routes of Spanish explorers and the establishment of towns by the Spanish. It's a short walk to the Planetarium, which shows how early explorers found their routes by celestial navigation and offers an opportunity to see what the night sky looked like without the light pollution of modern cityscapes.

Living history exhibits at the outdoor Timucua Indian Exhibit show how the Timucua lived, hunted, and cooked on this site for an estimated three thousand years. You may also witness the firing of a Spanish-era cannon and other demonstrations by costumed interpreters.

The First Encounter Exhibit explores the cultural exchanges between the Timucua and the Spanish, the basis of the cultural complexity of modern St. Augustine. Through artifacts found on the grounds of the park, the Archaeology Exhibit provides insight into the Timucuans' pottery and lifestyle, as well as their first encounters with Europeans. Here and at the Mission Nombre de Dios site next door, archaeologists have uncovered numerous items from the first contact period, including Timucuan artifacts, lead musket shot, pieces of porcelain and pottery, pins, buttons, iron nails, rosary beads, weapon fragments, and amulets and rings. These items help document the fact that the village of Seloy stood at this spot and that the first Spanish explorers settled here.

Mission Nombre de Dios

The Catholic Church established the Mission Nombre de Dios, or "Name of God Mission," as a Christian landmark. More broadly— and more certainly—the Mission grounds memorialize the founding of the first permanent Christian church in the country. The different shrines represent the various rites of Catholic worship identified with Florida's settlers from Spain, Greece, and Mexico. The modern Roman Catholic Church recognizes the Byzantine Rite Catholics and other Catholic groups as part of the broader Christian Church, traced back to St. Peter. The varied shrines reflect that recognition.

Archaeological digs on the Mission grounds have uncovered evidence of the first Spanish fortifications and Native American shell middens left by the Timucuan villagers of Seloy. The sheer size of some of the middens testified to the extended occupation of the site by large populations, with millions of oyster and other shells piled high.

Archaeology is supported by historical documents in some cases. Fleet chaplain Father Francisco López de Mendoza Grajales made note of the first construction of the fortifications around the longhouse at Seloy:

> They went ashore and were well-received
> by the Indians, who gave them a very large
> house of a cacique which is on the riverbank.
> And then Captains Patiño and San Vicente,

with strong industry and diligence, ordered a
ditch and moat made around the house, with
a rampart of earth and faggots. . . .

The replica rustic altar stands on the approximate spot of the
original Mass of Thanksgiving. Today visitors use the altar for
special events, such as the celebration of Mass during pilgrimages
and weddings. Every year, on the Saturday closest to September 8,
celebrants reenact the landing of Menéndez, followed by a Mass that
replicates the first Mass at St. Augustine.

The Mission Nombre de Dios, named by Menéndez himself,
remained part of the St. Augustine community well into the 1700s.
During the last sixty years of the First Spanish Period, church fathers
and parishioners funded several other local chapels. Menéndez
assigned Father López to be in charge of the Mission, making him
the first parish priest in the United States.

The Mission Nombre de Dios was the motherhouse for the
four "provinces" of missions, with nearly two hundred local mission
centers, or *doctrinas,* throughout what is now the Southeast. These
mission centers provided religious education and instruction in
European crafts and agriculture. At the same time, they became
village centers and military outposts that, although only lightly
fortified, helped deter English incursions from the north until the
eighteenth century.

Walking Tour Highlights of Mission Nombre de Dios

You encounter a fountain in a circled entranceway when you drive in
or leave a tour trolley. Off to the right of the circle stands the Prince of
Peace Church, built in 1965 to mark four hundred years of Catholic
presence in the United States. Reflecting the Cold War concerns of
the era, visitors often lit votive candles and offered prayers to prevent
a nuclear war. In addition, just inside the church is a chapel dedicated

to Our Lady of Fatima, the vision of Mary that appeared to three children in Fatima, Portugal, in 1917, warning that more world wars would occur without the consecration of Russia.

Next to the church is the Mission Nombre de Dios Museum, opened in 2010. The museum displays the original casket of Pedro Menéndez, made in 1574. Authorities disinterred his body in 1924 and sent it to Avilés, Spain, for reburial, but the casket remained here. The museum also houses artifacts uncovered on the Mission grounds by University of Florida archaeologists. Other displays include replicas of historical documents, coquina stones from older church structures, and a fifteen-minute documentary showing a reenactment of the 1565 founding of St. Augustine and telling the story of the Menéndez casket.

The self-guided tour from the Prince of Peace Church takes you across the Michael Gannon Bridge to an eleven-foot-tall bronze statue of Father López. Mounted on a coral and dark green granite base, the sculpture was carved by Dr. Ivan Mestrovic, who attended the dedication of the statue in 1958. Considered the greatest Croatian sculptor of the twentieth century, Mestrovic was Dean of Art at Notre Dame University while he worked on the sculpture.

You then pass near the 208-foot-tall steel cross commissioned in the 1960s by the Bishop (later Archbishop) of St. Augustine, Joseph P. Hurley. The Archbishop of Madrid, Casimiro Morcillo, dedicated the cross in October 1966 during the celebration of the four hundredth anniversary of the founding of St. Augustine and its first Catholic mission.

Set on a base of granite slabs and constructed of two hundred steel panels, the impressive cross weighs some seventy tons. To withstand hurricane-strength winds, the bottom sixty-five feet of the structure are filled with concrete. Floodlights make the cross visible

This footbridge, named after historian Michael Gannon, connects the Prince of Peace Church with the shrines and monuments near the waterfront.

The statue of Father López de Mendoza Grajales, the first priest in St. Augustine, stands near the waterfront at the Mission Nombre de Dios.

A bronze plaque on the Mission grounds details the locations of dozens of Catholic missions established by the Spanish throughout greater Florida.

from much of St. Augustine at night.

Just south of the cross, a bronze plaque lists many of the missions built by the Spanish in the Colonial Period up to 1763. The plaque shows the original missions, including the most northerly one set up by the Jesuits near Chesapeake Bay. After an interval during which laypeople held services, Franciscan missionaries took over the development of missions in 1578 and continued doing so until the arrival of the British, who put a stop to the Catholic missionary effort.

This small shrine on the Mission grounds honors the Mexican vision of the Virgin Mary and includes Aztec symbols such as the sun and moon.

Shrine of Our Lady of Guadalupe

The Shrine of Our Lady of Guadalupe, with its illustration in Spanish tiles, commemorates the 1531 vision of the Virgin Mary to Juan Diego in Guadalupe, Mexico. The image of Mary was imprinted by rose petals on Juan Diego's cloak when he showed the cloak to the local bishop.

Our Lady of Perpetual Help

Still another small shrine on the Mission Nombre de Dios grounds is devoted to Our Lady of Perpetual Help and represents the faith of Greek Byzantine Rite Catholics, many of whom make semiannual pilgrimages to the Mission to visit the shrine.

Our Lady of La Leche

Housed in its own small chapel, Our Lady of La Leche represents the Spanish version of veneration of the Virgin Mary. In the 1600s, prominent St. Augustine families formed a "confraternity," or group of laypeople, to raise funds to build the shrine.

Governor Hita y Salazar ordered the chapel built in 1677. It was destroyed twice in the eighteenth century during raids by the

The Chapel of Our Lady of Leche at the Mission Nombre de Dios Park is the site of pilgrimages and devotions of expectant mothers.

British. In 1915 private donations funded the current, ivy-covered replica. Pilgrims still visit the chapel, praying for the safe delivery of newborns.

Archaeology and History

In 2011 University of Florida archaeologists discovered the ninety-by-forty-foot-large foundation of a building from the late seventeenth century. They also discovered a sixteenth-century moat located close to the rustic altar. A posted notice points out that the moat might be the ditch built under the direction of Menéndez and noted by Father Lopez as the Spanish fortified their first encampment in Seloy. The moat ran from the shoreline, west about one hundred feet inland along the south side of the rustic altar replica.

Near the shoreline, a 2009 dig uncovered a Spanish limekiln, structured as a pit lined with logs. To make lime, workers would shovel oyster shells into the pit and burn them, producing lime, which could then be used for plaster, mortar, or whitewash. Researchers have never identified another pre-1650 limekiln in all of North America.

Fort Menendez at Old Florida Museum

At 259 San Marco Avenue, a few blocks north of the Fountain of Youth Park, stands Fort Menendez. The facility features cannon barrels and the masts of a "shipwreck" that loom over a stockade wall that faces San Marco Avenue. This is a great place for children to learn about the history of St. Augustine.

The facility first opened in 1996 as the Historic Villages of St. Augustine, operated by Charles F. Ponce Jr., a descendent of the Ponce and Solana families of St. Augustine. Ponce's vision was to make the history of St. Augustine come alive for children through hands-on learning and play. The same philosophy continued under new management in 2012.

You embark on a tour with a costumed interpreter-guide. The Spanish Village houses the governor's hacienda, and the Indian Village includes a replica council house and chief's hut with displays of Native American artifacts, a fish-drying rack, and a dugout canoe hollowed out by charring the inside. (Children can experience digging in charcoal.) Children and adults learn how to grind corn, make tabby (an oyster-shell mixture for building), and play early colonial games. Other experiences include making candles, grinding sugarcane, and writing with a quill pen. New exhibits center on ships and sailors and life in a Spanish fort.

At Fort Menendez, tour groups for children highlight different themes: the Timucua Indians, the First Spanish Period, and the American Territorial Period. Other programs center on Florida Cracker pioneers, black history, and an archeological dig.

With interactive displays like this dugout canoe, children and adults experience history at Fort Menendez, just a few blocks north of the original site of Seloy village on San Marco Avenue.

Chapter 2
THE FIRST SPANISH PERIOD
1565–1763

The Castillo and City Survival
Even though Menéndez founded the city in 1565, the only structure built before 1700 that still stands is the Castillo de San Marcos itself. Numerous other buildings erected later have survived, due to the protection offered by the Castillo and other defensive walls and forts.

Sir Francis Drake led the first of the four major attacks on the city in 1586. Another raid led by the privateer Robert Searle in 1668 finally convinced the Spanish to build the Castillo.

Building the Castillo, 1672–1695
The city needed strong leadership in Spain to provide a strengthened defense in the face of raids by Drake, Searle, and others. Acting as regent, Mariana, the mother of three-year-old Prince (later King) Carlos II of Spain, took charge.

On the grounds of the Castillo de San Marcos, the reconstructed Cubo Line shows how the city was protected by walls during the Spanish Colonial Period.

Church and Crown

While the Spanish Crown was concerned with military defense, the Church wanted to convert all of the natives in the New World to Christianity and to preserve Catholicism on the frontier. The Church and Crown worked side by side but not always comfortably. Furthermore, the parish priests did not always see eye to eye with the Franciscan monks. In 1690 the Franciscans refused to allow the priests into the courtyard of their monastery (now the St. Francis Barracks) for a funeral service for the wife of former governor Hita y Salazar. Governor Quiroga intervened and forced the monks to agree to the funeral ceremony.

The division of authority in St. Augustine and elsewhere throughout the Spanish Empire is evident in the city's surviving structures: convents, monasteries, missions, and Church-run hospitals among the armories, forts, walls, and guardhouses set up by the Crown and manned by the military.

Regent Mariana ordered the viceroy of New Spain (Mexico) to dispatch troops to St. Augustine, bringing the soldier strength there to the full complement of three hundred. She also had the viceroy help fund improvements to St. Augustine's fortifications.

Florida's Governor Manuel de Çendoya personally went to Havana, Cuba, in search of stonemasons and other craftsmen to work on a proposed new fort. There he recruited the military engineer Ignazio Daza to design the fort. Daza's plans followed the outline of the older wooden fort but was built of masonry using locally mined coquina.

Local supervisors assembled materials and a workforce, beginning construction in 1672. The work continued for twenty-three years, following Daza's plans long after he died. The Castillo de San Marcos withstood two serious sieges, deterred others, and never fell in battle, serving as a monument to Daza's brilliance and Mariana's leadership.

Quarry

The Old Coquina Quarry, where laborers mined the fort's material, is located just inside the Anastasia Island State Park entrance. Workers cut the huge blocks loose, carried them by oxen to barges, then floated them across the Matanzas River that separates Anastasia Island from the city and stacked them at the work site. You can visit the quarry today, but the overgrown area gives only a faint impression of the former works. A few interpretive signs help you understand the mining process, however.

In 1702, during Queen Anne's War, Governor James Moore of Carolina destroyed St. Augustine, with the exception of the Castillo. Georgia Governor James Oglethorpe led a large force of British and Native American troops to attack the city in 1740. Again, the massive fortress survived the invasion.

On the terreplein, or top level, of the Castillo de San Marcos, authentic cannons loom beneath the Burgundy Cross flag of Spain.

Defenses Enhanced: African Militia and Fort Mose

The Castillo de San Marcos and city walls alone could not stop every invasion, however. The Spanish needed troops elsewhere in the empire, so the Crown set a quota of three hundred men at the lonely outpost, not enough to deter a major attack. A policy of sanctuary provided a partial solution to the manpower problem.

The policy had its origin in 1687, when eleven fugitive African slaves from Charleston, South Carolina, fled to Florida by boat. Florida Governor Diego de Quiroga y Losado ordered that they be given sanctuary from recapture and re-enslavement and baptized as Catholics. When the English sought the return of the fugitives, Governor Diego refused their request. To back up this local policy, King Carlos II freed all slaves who fled to the colony by a 1693 proclamation.

During the invasion of Florida led by Governor Oglethorpe of Georgia, the African militia at Fort Mose put up a stiff resistance, then retreated to the safety of the Castillo. The African-born commander of the black troops, Francisco Menéndez, had fled from South Carolina to Florida in 1724 under the sanctuary policy.

To recapture Mose, Menéndez led a raid of the black troops from the Castillo early in the morning of June 26, 1740. They surprised and expelled the British forces. Sixty-eight British soldiers were killed and thirty-four were captured in the engagement. The Spanish lost only two men. A photo plaque at present-day Fort Mose State Park shows the bloody fight. Oglethorpe then stationed his forces on Anastasia Island and bombarded the Castillo and city with cannon fire. The townspeople and Spanish soldiers—nearly two thousand people—took refuge in the Castillo. New bombproof shelters along the fort walls proved good protection against the relatively small caliber of the English artillery.

By August 6, 1740, Oglethorpe had withdrawn the last of his forces, sending them by ship back to Charleston. After the British retreat, Francisco Menéndez led the African militia back to the

---

War of Jenkins' Ear

One attack on St. Augustine resulted from a cut-off ear. On April 9, 1731, a Spanish patrol sloop, the *San Antonio,* intercepted a British merchant brig, the *Rebecca,* off Havana. The Spanish authorities examined the brig's papers and cargo and discovered the ship was used for smuggling. *Rebecca*'s captain, Robert Jenkins, insulted the Spanish captain, Juan de Leon Fandino. In response, de Leon cut off one of Jenkins' ears with a sword. According to Jenkins, de Leon then said, "Were the King of England here and also in violation of the laws, I would do the same to him!"

Jenkins returned to England and in 1738 reported the incident to a committee of the House of Commons, showing them his preserved ear. Shocked, the British demanded retribution. The resulting war, brewing for years over disputed land, pitted the new British colony of Georgia, first founded in 1733, against the nearly seventy-year-old colony of Spanish St. Augustine.

---

site of Mose, where they built a second fort and a little town just northeast of the original site. The second Fort Mose thrived during the 1740s and 1750s. In recent years, archaeologists and historians have established that by 1759, the village consisted of twenty-two palm huts with a population of about sixty-seven people.

At the end of the First Spanish Period in 1763, Menéndez and the black settlers at Mose evacuated to Cuba and settled in Ceiba Mocha, now a suburb of Havana. The abandoned Fort Mose site slowly vanished, although for years it served as a favorite picnic retreat for St. Augustine residents. The waters of the marsh isolated the two fort sites in recent decades.

Most of the Spanish also left at the end of the first Colonial Period, moving to New Spain and Cuba. On January 21, 1764, the last Spanish ship left. At least ten Spanish subjects and their families, together with a number of mestizo families, decided not to evacuate on the departing ships. The First Spanish Period ended with a small settlement at St. Augustine.

SITES TO SEE

Despite the Spanish evacuation, many eighteenth-century homes and commercial and government structures remained standing. British troops had stripped wooden doors and shutters for firewood, but the masonry buildings that had not been gutted by fire remained and were gradually repaired and maintained during the following decades. Those buildings survived because of the protection provided by the three forts: Castillo de San Marcos, Fort Mose, and Fort Matanzas.

In this section, we describe sites in three groups. A walking tour of the city takes you to sites that reflect different aspects of the First Spanish Period: Castillo de San Marcos; Cubo Wall and Santo Domingo Redoubt; St. George Street; Spanish Colonial Village; Plaza and Government House; and the Oldest House. A second group consists of three out-of-town sites—each a short drive from the city—that reflect the turbulent military history of the First Spanish Period: Fort Mose, Oglethorpe Battery Park, and Fort Matanzas. The third group consists of three modern commercial attractions that relate to the theme of pirate attacks and appeal to both children and adults: The Pirate Museum; the Pirate Fashions N Fotos; and the Black Raven Pirate Ship.

Castillo de San Marcos

Originally built between 1672 and 1695, the massive Castillo dominates the city's waterfront. Maintained by the United States Park Service, the fortress features the original military architecture of the seventeenth century. Outside the fort, a masonry wall supports the earthen rampart facing the moat. The layout exposed any attackers on foot to cannon fire from the fort. Inside, costumed interpreters in authentic Spanish military attire regularly march up the artillery ramp to present demonstrations of cannon firing. Between performances, they stand guard in the lower courtyard and answer questions.

Sites to see include the heavily arched and bombproof casemate rooms surrounding the parade ground. On the terreplein, or roof level, a display of cannons includes some from the seventeenth century and others captured from Spain in the Spanish-American War of 1898.

At the corners, or bastions, of the fort, four sentry towers with vertical slot openings stand guard. The loophole slots, wider on the inside than on the outside, offered only a very small target to attackers.

Displays in the fort were developed by Park Service historians and present its rich history of construction and defense. The fortress lets you immerse yourself in detailed knowledge of fortification

Heavy weapons and ammunition could be hauled up this sloped ramp to the terreplein for emplacement. The original Castillo plan by the military engineer Ignazio Daza has stood the test of time.

engineering, seventeenth-century labor conditions, styles and methods of warfare, and the larger history of St. Augustine. The bookshop carries works that provide even more information.

Builders of the Castillo used the locally quarried sedimentary stone called coquina. Millions of packed seashells make up coquina; the term derives from the Spanish for "little shell." Archaeologists have determined that local St. Augustine residents used coquina before the fort was built. Digs have uncovered coquina in wells and parts of buildings since the early 1600s. Using coquina in the fort turned out to be a stroke of genius. The coquina walls could withstand cannon and musket fire. Rather than shattering when hit by a cannon ball, the relatively soft material absorbed the shot.

Cubo Wall and Santo Domingo Redoubt

Just two blocks to the west of the Castillo, a reconstruction of the Cubo Wall and the Santo Domingo Redoubt shows how the builders constructed defensive walls during the Spanish Colonial Period. The redoubt reconstruction is located on Orange Street, bordering the parking lot behind the visitors center.

Built in 1704, the original Cubo Wall protected the town from attack from the north, serving as the last line of defense of the city. The term *cubo* referred to rounded or pointed bastions built into the wall. The wall originally had three *cubos,* or redoubts. A graph at the Santo Domingo redoubt reconstruction shows the *cubo* fortification profile, with firing step, parapet, face, berm, moat, and glacis (the sloped approach). The original Rosario Line ran roughly parallel to the San Sebastian River, started at the Cubo Line at about this point, and then ran south, curving into the Matanzas River at about where Bridge Street now runs.

St. George Street

As you stroll down the pedestrian-only St. George Street, you will notice historical markers on many of the buildings. Throughout the city, researchers have identified more than thirty homes from the Colonial Periods. Even though many date in whole or in part to the years before 1763, several of them have been restored and furnished to represent later eras and are discussed in later chapters. Some recent owners have converted surviving historic structures of the First Spanish Period to modern, alternate uses, such as shops and residences. Along the street, plaques describe the histories of buildings such as these: Biassou House, now occupied by Whetstone Chocolates; the circa-1740 De Mesa Sánchez House, part of the Old Spanish Quarter; the 1749 Casa Avero, now the home of the Photios

With overhanging balconies and many shops, this section of Hypolita Street just east of St. George Street shows the comfortable combination of history and commerce found in St. Augustine today.

St. George Street Houses

The historic homes and other structures on St. George Street include some built during the First Spanish, British, and Second Spanish Periods. Several buildings are reconstructions following the original plans, often including original walls. Most have been modified over the years. You can read details on the historic plaques affixed to the buildings. Some of the most noteworthy are listed here in approximate north-to-south order:

House	Number	Era
Oldest Wooden School	14	2nd Spanish
Spanish Quarter Village:		
Gomez House	27	1st Spanish
Florencia House	33	1st Spanish
De Mesa-Sanchez House	43	2nd Spanish & U.S.
Houses:		
Photios Shrine/Avero	41	1st Spanish
Joseph Salcedo		
(Gen. Biassou House)	42	2nd Spanish
Arrivas	46	British, 2nd Spanish, U.S.
Rodriguez-Avero-Sanchez	52	1st, 2nd Spanish, U.S.
Benet Store	62	2nd Spanish
Oliveros	59	2nd Spanish
Benet	65	2nd Spanish
Suarez-McHenry	69	1st Spanish
Ortega	70	1st Spanish
Marin-Hasset	97	1st Spanish
Sanchez-Burt	105	2nd Spanish
Peña Peck	143	1st Spanish

Shrine; and the 1750 Peña-Peck House, now the headquarters of the Women's Exchange.

When you walk along St. George, Marine, and Charlotte Streets and look past the electrical lines, commercial signs, and parked cars, the eighteenth century still shows through. The First Spanish Period residences, stuccoed masonry walls, interior patios, and overhanging wooden balconies echo St. Augustine before 1763. Here stand structures built or modified in four different centuries, from the 1700s through the present. The earliest era, the First Spanish Period, is represented by at least six different buildings along St. George Street, as shown in the sidebar.

Colonial Spanish Quarter

Located at 35 St. George Street, the Colonial Spanish Quarter operates as a living history museum, with workshops and costumed interpreters who present life during the First Spanish Period. The small, simulated community, administered by the City of St. Augustine Department of Heritage Tourism, presents a variety of programs centering around early Spanish Colonial life. In recent years, the Spanish Quarter has undergone reorganization, and the exhibits have been modified.

At the Colonial Spanish Quarter, interpreters provide glimpses into colonial life. John Powell demonstrates the nearly lost art of penmanship.

Plaza de la Constitución

At the southern end of St. George Street lies the town plaza. The first formal plan of the city was established by royal ordinances under Governor Gonzalo Méndez de Cancio y Donlebún in the late 1500s. Laid out in a rectangle, the plaza measures one and a half times long as it is wide.

A stroll through the plaza takes you past the historic marketplace, a simple, open-sided, roofed structure typical of many such city markets throughout Latin America in the 1600s and 1700s. Although

In the Plaza de la Constitución, the roofed, open-air market and the well are reconstructions of Spanish Period features.

hurricanes destroyed the original market shelter more than once, the replica follows the original lines. For many years, the market displayed a sign that read "Old Slave Market," but records suggest it served as more of a general marketplace. Slave sales were characteristic of the later period when St. Augustine was under U.S. control. Nearby, a public well provided fresh water in the 1600s and later.

Government House

On the west side of St. George Street between Cathedral Place and King Street, the Government House faces the plaza. This modern building replicates the facade of the structure originally built in 1710 and stands on the site that housed the homes and offices of all of the colonial governors. The Spanish built the original Government House as part of the reconstruction of the city following the English raid of 1702.

This 1930s replica represents the Government House, which served as the governors' residence and as the capitol building for all of Florida during the First Spanish Period.

The Works Progress Administration (WPA) built the replica in 1935, incorporating some of the original walls. The new Government House then served for a period as the central U.S. Post Office for St. Augustine.

In 1964 the State of Florida converted the building into the headquarters for local historic preservation. Since 1991 the first-floor museum has spelled out the story of St. Augustine from prehistoric times to the present. The displays include archaeological finds, a mock-up of a Colonial-era ship cargo hold, and a range of artifacts. A tour of the museum offers a solid introduction to the whole history of St. Augustine, with displays explaining construction details, shipping, military defense, and other details.

The Oldest House

Five blocks south of the plaza, at 14 St. Francis Street, you can get a glimpse of civilian life in Colonial St. Augustine at the Oldest House museum complex. Owned and operated by the St. Augustine Historical Society, the complex includes the house, two separate museums, an exhibition gallery, a traditional ornamental garden, and a museum store.

The Oldest House, also known as the González-Alvarez House, is one of the oldest still-standing Spanish Colonial residences in Florida. Parts of several other houses in St. Augustine, including the O'Reilly House, have been traced to the late 1600s. This site had a home on it prior to the burning of the city during James Moore's raid in 1702. The present house dates to the period of reconstruction following Queen Anne's War (1702–1713).

The house became a landmark site in St. Augustine in the nineteenth century, when visitors began touring it. On April 15, 1970, the U.S. Department of the Interior named the house a national

The Oldest House Museum and Gardens provide physical documentation for nearly five hundred years of St. Augustine history.

historic landmark. A detached, eighteenth-century–style kitchen shows how cooks prepared meals during the Colonial Era.

Opened in 1924, the Manucy Museum in the Webb Building was the first building in the state of Florida designed and built as a museum. The museum explores how the Oldest House fits into the story of St. Augustine, covering exploration, settlement, Christian missions, and the Spanish galleons. Displays show early trade and commerce, as well as the later eras of railroad and auto tourism, land booms, and the development of resorts and attractions in modern Florida. Presentations cover 500 years of Florida history and 450 years of St. Augustine history.

The St. Augustine Historical Society also maintains the Page L. Edwards Gallery, located on the first floor of the Dunham Building. The gallery features rotating exhibitions of materials drawn from the Historical Society's larger collections and brings in traveling exhibits from other museums. The Dunham Building houses the St. Augustine Historical Society's offices.

Cofradia Well

Returning north to the Plaza along Aviles Street, you will spot a quiet, small park with a well on the corner of Bravo Lane. A marker describes the site of a well thought to have originally been dug between 1614 and 1657. Archeologists found that the well had been filled with chunks of coquina and other building materials from a destroyed building. In 1764 the Confraternity of the Blessed Sacrament, a layperson organization, owned the site. Research has yet to uncover the details of the destruction that led to the filling of the well.

New York tourist Colleen McEvoy-Folley takes a break in front of the Cofradia Well.

RELATED, OUT-OF-TOWN SITES
*Three sites related to the British-Spanish War of Jenkins' Ear—Fort Mose,
Oglethorpe Park, and Fort Matanzas—are short drives from the center
of town. These spots offer further physical documentation of the events
surrounding the British effort to conquer Florida in the 1740s.*

Fort Mose
Two miles north of the Castillo de San Marcos, a small visitors center
and museum commemorates Fort Mose, situated on Fort Mose Road,
off highway A1A. You can't explore the archaeological dig itself that
turned up details of Fort Mose, but you can view the site from a
boardwalk that stretches out into the marshland. In the distance, two
overgrown hammocks mark the spots of the first and second fortress

*Two miles north of the city, the original outer wall crossed the road at this point.
Just to the east is the African-American Fort Mose, which anchored this defensive
line in the eighteenth century.*

communities occupied by Spanish-African militiamen who effectively resisted the invaders under General James Oglethorpe in 1740.

The museum in the visitors center features changing displays of artifacts found at the site, dioramas and depictions of life in the community, and a short video about the Mose story. The museum hosts many visits from children's groups learning about the country's African-American heritage, attested to by changing selections of crayon drawings.

At the intersection of Fort Mose Road and Highway A1A, a short section of reconstructed Mose Wall, with gateposts, represents this outer defense line of the city. The wall and gate towers give an impression of the defensive perimeter that helped ward off attacks on St. Augustine from the north.

Oglethorpe Park

Travel across the Bridge of Lions to Anastasia Island and you'll find Oglethorpe Park. Located on Arredondo Avenue between Oglethorpe Boulevard and Alcazar Street, it could be just another neighborhood park with bike racks, lawns, and walkways. It hardly seems the site of great historic events. A marker shows the spot where General James Oglethorpe mounted his artillery battery to bombard St. Augustine and the Castillo from June 27 to July 20, 1740. Standing on this spot, you get a better idea of why the artillery attack on the fortress and town petered out. The battery of guns had to fire about half a mile to reach the Castillo, and the small cannonballs from wheeled artillery pieces did little damage at that range.

Fort Matanzas

Fifteen miles south of the city on Anastasia Island, not far from the spot of the massacres of the French in 1565, the Spanish constructed a fort to protect the approach to St. Augustine by water from the south. Park rangers at Fort Matanzas National Monument provide a free boat ride out to the fort during daylight hours.

Governor Manuel de Montiano ordered work to begin on this coquina fortress to guard the inlet at Matanzas. The work started in the fall of 1740, with coquina dug from a quarry at El Piñon, south of Matanzas. The construction involved driving piles into the soft marshland as a foundation for the heavy coquina blocks.

In September 1742 and April 1743, Oglethorpe attempted attacks from the sea through the inlet but encountered the newly built Fort Matanzas. Shots from the fort's cannons drove off the

This small fort at Matanzas Inlet was built in the 1740s. The only entrance was by ladder.

At Fort Matanzas, a few small cannons guarded the waterway approach to the city from the south.

A few cannons protected the inlet from the small ships that could cross the sandbars, such as sloops and schooners. The guns on display had a range of up to three miles, more than enough to stave off would-be invaders. In the nineteenth century, the fort fell into disrepair, with severe cracks in the walls and large bushes growing from the crevices. Old photographs on display at the shore-side visitors center show the ruins before twentieth-century restoration work.

COMMERCIAL ATTRACTIONS

Several commercial enterprises in modern St. Augustine reflect the theme of piracy and privateers. For visitors with children, these attractions help develop an understanding of the history behind the popular myths about piracy.

Pirate and Treasure Museum

The Pirate and Treasure Museum was founded by Pat Croce, an avid collector of pirate memorabilia and artifacts. A modest sign marks the entrance at 12 Castillo Drive, just a few blocks north of the plaza, facing the harbor.

Croce's career has included a term as president of the Philadelphia 76ers basketball team. He has been an author, business owner, and reality television show judge. His latest book, *The Pirate Handbook: A Rogue's Guide to Pillage and Plunder, Chaos and Conquest,* is one of several on piracy and modern business methods.

The Pirate and Treasure Museum was established by Pat Croce, who houses some of his piracy artifacts here.

The museum allows you to visit the Golden Age of Piracy in the early eighteenth century, starting with the cobbled streets of Port Royal, Jamaica, where pirates often took refuge and spent their ill-gotten gains. The Rogue's Tavern simulates the off-hours of pirate life. The Main Deck offers a battle scene, and on the Gun Deck, you can fire a real miniature cannon. The Captain's Cabin displays the pirate flag and William Kidd's journal. The museum provides an impressionistic way to explore how old-time piracy has become romanticized and fictionalized and why it remains fascinating.

Host of the independent Pirate Fashions N Fotos, Bill Lee shows off one of his pirate costumes.

Pirate Fashions N Fotos

The only old-time photo studio with a focus on the pirate theme operates just around the corner at 26 Cuna Street. Open since 2008, this unique little shop sells pirate paraphernalia, including authentic clothing, replica and black-powder firing weapons, swords, and knives. In addition, you can dress up in pirate garb and have a professional photo taken.

Black Raven Pirate Ship

Several times daily, this motorized replica of a sailing ship sets sail for two-hour cruises from a dock near the foot of King Street, just south of the Bridge of Lions. You can choose from adults-only cruises and those designed for parents and children. A fully stocked bar and an announcement that those aboard may be the only pirates to accept credit cards give you a sense of the entertainment aboard. Costumed staff, including pirate wenches, lead you in skits, songs, and an attempt to find your "inner pirate."

Chapter 3
THE BRITISH PERIOD
1763–1783

The British took possession of Florida in 1763 as a result of what Americans call the Seven Years' War. The British had captured Havana, Cuba, and in the peace treaty ending the war, Spain exchanged Florida for the return of Havana to Spanish control.

In 1763, just before the British took over, the Spanish population of Florida was about seven thousand. Nearly all of these residents left for Cuba after the British took possession, rejecting British offers to remain. Only a few families stayed on in St. Augustine. Their descendants represented a core of Spanish families in the city: Sanchez, Solana, Ponce de León, Espinosa, Canto, de Aguilar, Salgado, de Almo, and de Herrera.

The British divided Florida into two colonies, East and West Florida. Pensacola became the capital of West Florida, and St. Augustine continued as the colonial capital of East Florida. The city became the social and administrative center for the whole settled region along the St. Johns River in what is now northeastern Florida.

New settlers arrived—primarily British planters from colonies to the north or from the West Indies—and established plantations in East Florida. The British granted millions of acres of land to wealthy investors from Britain and Europe, to planters from South Carolina and Georgia, and, toward the end of the period, to Loyalists who fled from the United States during the American Revolution.

Governor James Grant

James Grant, a Scots military officer in the British Army, had served in the siege of Havana during the French and Indian War. The British Crown rewarded him with an appointment as the first governor of British Florida. Grant arrived in St. Augustine in August 1763 and

Indigo

Indigo is a deep-blue–violet dye derived from the plant *indigofera*, originally grown in India. By the Colonial period, indigo was raised throughout the tropics and widely used in West Africa, where workers perfected the art of extracting the dye from the harvested plants and dyeing cloth. Since the dye wasn't water soluble and was therefore colorfast, it was highly desirable. The process of growing, harvesting, and refining the dye was labor intensive and disagreeable, however—the harvested plant had to ferment, giving off a horrible odor—and the work was performed by slaves or indentured servants.

During Florida's British Period, Governors James Grant and Patrick Tonyn personally established huge, profitable indigo plantations near St. Augustine. Indigo prices collapsed after the American Revolution due to international competition, however, and planters shifted to other crops.

officially took office on October 31. Over the course of Grant's eight-year administration and those of his successors, Acting Governor John Moultrie (1771–74) and Governor Patrick Tonyn (1774–84), the British allotted some 2,856,000 acres in 114 plantations. Owners established plantations across northeast Florida, some several days' travel from St. Augustine, which became the commercial and lively social center of the larger region of outlying plantations.

New Smyrna Plantation

Even though it was located seventy miles to the south of St. Augustine, a large, indentured-servant plantation at New Smyrna became an important part of the city's social history. Unlike the African slaves at the plantations of Grant, Tonyn, and the other planters, the workers at New Smyrna didn't evacuate Florida at the end of the British period. Their story resulted from the ambitious plan of a Scots doctor named Andrew Turnbull.

Dr. Turnbull brought more than one thousand workers to Florida. Recruited in Greece, Italy, Corsica, and the Spanish Mediterranean island of Minorca (then under British rule), the men and women were assembled for transport to Florida. Many of the bachelors he recruited in Greece married local Minorcan women. The whole group became known as Minorcans, who spoke the native Catalan language.

In 1768 Turnbull sailed to his land grant, naming it after Smyrna, then a Greek city and the birthplace of his wife. He established the largest British-owned plantation, in terms of numbers of workers, in all of North America. The workers signed indentures to work without pay for a set number of years, usually between five and eight. They planted, harvested, and processed indigo. After their terms expired, they would be released as free men and women with land grants.

Although they hailed from the Mediterranean and were more accustomed to hot summers than northern Europeans, the workers encountered stifling humidity as well as terrible food, corporal punishment, and imprisonment. Mosquitoes so notoriously infested the area that the Spanish had named the inlet at New Smyrna *Los Mosquitos*. About half of the original settlers were lost at sea or succumbed to malaria or starvation.

Turnbull ordered his overseers to torture the servants into signing on for additional years before their original terms expired. By 1777 a few escapees from New Smyrna and concerned Spanish and British residents of St. Augustine pleaded with Governor Tonyn to intervene at the plantation. Since Tonyn disliked Turnbull anyway, he felt inclined to believe the reports.

In July 1777, Tonyn needed forces to guard Florida against possible invasion by Americans during the War of Independence. So he freed the surviving New Smyrna settlers, numbering some six hundred, including children born on the plantation. Evicted from the plantation by Turnbull, the survivors walked overland to St. Augustine.

Governor Tonyn allotted small grants of land to the survivors. Within a few years, the freed Minorcans prospered, raising crops, livestock, and children under the leadership of Father Pedro Camps.

Governor Tonyn

Patrick Tonyn (1725–1804) served as second colonial governor of British East Florida from 1775 to 1783. On appointment, Tonyn received a twenty-thousand-acre tract of land south of Black Creek on the St. Johns River. After arriving in March 1774, he was given an additional 125-acre land grant, and he bought a town lot and three thousand acres of rural land. On the Black Creek plantation, he used slave labor to grow quality indigo.

During the American Revolution, British troops burned Tonyn's plantation to the ground to prevent Patriot forces from encamping there. Tonyn moved many of his slaves to St. Augustine to work on the city's defenses.

Father Pedro Camps

At the insistence of his wife, Gracia Dura Bin, Turnbull had allowed two Catholic clergymen to accompany the settlers from Minorca to New Smyrna. The Catholic Gracia wanted to ensure that the settlers had priests with them.

This statue on the grounds of the Cathedral, sculpted by Josel Vilanomay of Barcelona, Spain, documents the flight of the Minorcans from New Smyrna to St. Augustine. Father Pedro Camps holds the cross.

Turnbull selected Father Camps, a secular priest who hailed from the town of Mercadal on Minorca and was well respected there for his preaching. Both Camps and his colleague, Augustinian Brother Bartolome Casanovas, arrived with the servants as "apostolic missionaries," responsible for the spiritual life of their flock as well as their physical well-being. Turnbull had expelled Brother Casanovas because he complained of the servants' treatment. Father Camps was more diplomatic, but he recorded the details of the servants' lives.

When Governor Tonyn ordered the servants freed, Turnbull kept Father Camps a virtual prisoner for four months after the mass exodus from the plantation. When released, Camps joined the Minorcans in St. Augustine. The British had expelled all of the Spanish Catholic priests from the city, so Camps found no Catholic parish for the new arrivals. He established a chapel on the ground floor of a small house near the City Gates where he served as parish priest. That building, at 39/41 St. George Street, now houses the St. Photios Shrine and a small museum dedicated to the Minorcan story.

William Bartram

One of the early travelers to St. Augustine was the young naturalist William Bartram, who explored Florida, Georgia, the Carolinas, and Alabama in the period 1773–77.

A Quaker from Philadelphia whose father had been a royal botanist for King George III, William traveled alone, treating the Native Americans he encountered with respect. As a result, his safety was ensured and some called him Flower Hunter, as he continually collected new species of plants. Bartram later published his journal, *Travels of William Bartram*, which became a best seller in the North. Readers learned of St. Augustine and enjoyed his colorful descriptions of Florida plants, natives, and plantations.

Modern readers, however, find that Bartram romanticized both Native Americans and Southern plantation life in his widely read journal. For instance, he visited Turnbull's plantation and made no comment on the condition of the workers there, commenting instead on Turnbull's hospitality.

William Bartram painted this bird on his 1774 tour of florida. (Courtesy of the Library of Congress)

SITES TO SEE

Sites that pertain to the British Period are scattered through the city. This walking tour features sites that reflect various aspects of the years from 1763 to 1783.

Tolomato Cemetery

Father Camps established the Tolomato Cemetery in 1777 on the former site of a village named Tolomato. The cemetery is located two blocks west of St. George Street on Cordova Street. The Church had set up Tolomato for refugee Guale Indians, converted to Christianity by Franciscan monks in the First Spanish Period. A small cemetery on the grounds of the village had a separate section for black Catholics. The Tolomato village settlement in St. Augustine stood right outside the Rosario Line, the defensive wall lined with Spanish dagger plants that ran along the western edge of the city.

When the British took over St. Augustine in 1763, they demolished the small wooden Catholic church at the Tolomato village for firewood, leaving only the coquina bell tower. When William Bartram traveled through Florida in 1765, he noted that the bell tower in the Tolomato settlement still stood, although the original wooden church had been torn down. When the Minorcans arrived from New Smyrna in 1777, Father Camps petitioned the British governor for permission to use the mission site for the new arrivals. Soon the cemetery there became the burial grounds for the Minorcans who died in St. Augustine. Most of the Minorcans settled in the nearby blocks between the cemetery and the house on St. George Street that Camps used as a parish church.

When the Catholic Church ordered the Cathedral built in the 1790s, workers obtained coquina from the Tolomato church tower to use in the new building. Located close to the center of the city,

Built on the site of a village of refugee Guale Indians from Georgia, the Tolomato Cemetery contains the lost grave of General Georges Biassou.

the Tolomato Cemetery continued as a Catholic burial ground as the government of St. Augustine changed hands from England to Spain and then to the United States. Much later, in 1853, the diocese built the small mortuary chapel now at the rear of the cemetery. The cemetery remained in use until 1884.

The Tolomato Cemetery served as the burial place for several notable St. Augustinians, including Father Camps, Father Miguel O'Reilly, Father Félix Varela, and the first Bishop of St. Augustine, Augustin Verot. The Church removed Father Camps' body to the Cathedral grounds in the 1790s. Cuba later removed the body of Felix Varela, a hero of Cuban independence, to Havana. Bishop Verot's remains stayed at the small chapel in the rear of the cemetery.

St. Photios Greek Orthodox Shrine

The St. Photios Greek Orthodox National Shrine represents one of the best-presented and best-funded historic sites in St. Augustine. Originally built in 1749 and known as the Casa Avero, the building represents the British and Second Spanish Periods. Entering through the courtyard at 41 St. George Street, you discover the museum devoted to the New Smyrna story. The museum combines history with beautifully kept displays of the Greek Orthodox religion. A video entitled *Our Plymouth Rock* presents the story of the Greek immigrants and the New Smyrna experience. The Saint Photios Chapel displays dazzling Byzantine frescos of scenes from the life of Christ and images of apostles and saints. Historic markers across St. George Street amplify the story of the Minorcans from New Smyrna.

St. Francis Barracks

St. Francis Barracks, located along the waterfront at the corner of Marine and St. Francis Streets, faces the Matanzas River. The Order of St. Francis built the original barracks structure between 1724 and 1755 during the First Spanish Period. The Franciscan holy order had previously occupied several wooden structures for their monastery, but the fire set during the raid on the city in 1702 by the British destroyed their buildings. When the monks rebuilt, they used coquina. The monastery in St. Augustine served as headquarters for the mission effort throughout Florida.

When the British took over St. Augustine in 1763, the Franciscan monks departed and the British converted the monastery to a military barracks. It has housed military commands ever since. St. Francis Barracks encompasses the main building and several smaller surrounding structures, as well as the property along Marine Street associated with them.

When the British took over, they added a wooden barracks and the coquina King's Bakery. The King's Bakery has been identified

Military forces have occupied a structure on the site of the St. Francis Barracks since 1763.

as the only remaining structure in the city entirely built during the British Period.

When the United States acquired Florida in 1821, the main monastery building remained a barracks for troops. When the Confederacy controlled St. Augustine for just over a year from 1861 to 1862, local Confederate units occupied the structure, but they evacuated when U.S. Marines and Army troops reoccupied St. Augustine in 1863. The Army deactivated the barracks in 1900, but with complete restructuring, it has served as the headquarters for Florida National Guard units since then, the only U.S. military site named for a religious figure. The bakery building has been converted to a garage.

The King's Bakery is the only surviving structure in St. Augustine from the British Colonial Period. It was used to bake bread for British troops stationed at St. Francis Barracks.

The Tovar House and the Oldest House

Many of the buildings in St. Augustine have acquired family or personal names from one period even though they were constructed earlier and occupied by numerous other families. The Tovar House, now administered as part of the Oldest House complex, saw a typically long sequence of owners. At the end of the First Spanish Period, an infantryman named Jose Tovar lived in this building at the corner of St. Francis and Charlotte Streets.

The eighteenth century Tovar House is now part of the Oldest House complex and houses archeological finds.

During the British Period, Mary Evans and her husband, Sergeant Joseph Peavett, owned the Oldest House. They operated a tavern on the first floor. The novel *Maria* by Eugenia Price tells their story and that of Luciano de Herrera, the Spanish secret agent who remained in St. Augustine to keep the Spanish informed of military and strategic developments under the British authorities.

Eugenia Price

Eugenia Price (1916–1996) was a prolific author of historical, romantic, and inspirational books. Among her many works were three in the Florida Trilogy series: *Maria, Don Juan McQueen,* and *Margaret's Story,* which are based on historical Florida characters. Price enjoyed a lengthy career writing radio soap operas, thirteen major novels, and twenty-six nonfiction works. In her later years, she lived on St. Simon's Island, Georgia.

Scottish merchant John Johnson occupied the corner Tovar building next door to Mary Evans and Joseph Peavett. In 1784, at the beginning of the Second Spanish Period, a Canary Islander by the name of Jose Coruna lived in the Tovar House with his family. An assistant surgeon named Tomas Carabello also lived in the house.

Geronimo Alvarez, who owned the Oldest House after Evans and Peavett, purchased the corner building in 1791, and it remained in the Alvarez family until 1871. Today the Tovar House features archeological displays. This structure, like several others, echoes different periods of St. Augustine's history.

Chapter 4
THE SECOND SPANISH PERIOD
1784–1821

In the Treaty of Paris of 1783, Great Britain accepted the independence of the thirteen colonies and ceded Florida back to Spain. This transfer led to the second period of Spanish rule in St. Augustine from 1784 until 1821.

After the Spanish regained Florida, East Florida's population numbered about seventeen thousand, mostly Native Americans. Fewer than one thousand whites and two hundred free African-Americans lived in and around St. Augustine. Minorcans liberated from New Smyrna made up the majority of the whites. Some free African-Americans were left behind when the British planters left with their slaves. A few British families remained on the condition they swear loyalty to Spain and accept Catholicism. Most of the British, however, liquidated their holdings and properties at great financial loss and accepted transportation to loyal British colonies in the West Indies.

East Florida faced turmoil under Spanish rule during the next three decades. Conflict sprang from causes far beyond the borders of Florida, including the general collapse of the Spanish Empire in the New World that came with the dispute between Napoleon and the Bourbons for control of Spain.

With Spanish control weakened throughout the Spanish Empire, adventurers, smugglers, slave-traders, and pirates in Florida seized the opportunity to operate outside of Spanish law. A new and revived African militia provided one source of local military aid for the Spanish. Seminole Indian warriors, augmented by escaped African-American slaves from colonies to the north, represented another military force that the Spanish called upon.

Two Treaties

St. Augustine changed hands twice in the late 1700s. At the end of the French and Indian War in 1763, Spain ceded Florida, with its capital in St. Augustine, to Britain in the first Treaty of Paris. Spain regained Havana, Cuba, which had been seized by Britain during the war. During the American War of Independence (1775–1781), Florida remained in British hands, not joining the other thirteen colonies in the Revolution. But in a second Treaty of Paris, signed in 1783, Great Britain accepted independence of the thirteen colonies and ceded Florida back to Spain.

Both treaties allowed subjects of the former regime eighteen months to sell their real estate in Florida, recover their debts, and move out of the territory if they wanted to leave. A small group of old families remained through both treaties.

Outlaw Regimes

From 1795 to 1820, St. Augustine was threatened by lawless leaders and regions. Havens for outlaws and self-proclaimed rulers spread as Spanish control weakened. In West Florida, William Augustus Bowles, a loyalist from Maryland, set up the Muskogee Republic near present-day Tallahassee in the period 1799–1803.

Fugitive slaves established an enclave with British support in Spanish West Florida at the "Negro Fort," later the site of Fort Gadsden. U.S. troops and unauthorized invading forces of filibusters invaded both West and East Florida more than once, holding territories in the colony for short periods in 1795 and in 1812.

About seventy miles north of St. Augustine on Amelia Island, Scottish adventurer Gregor MacGregor established his own regime. His little "republic" was later taken over by Luis Aury, who claimed to rule in the name of independent Mexico. Both Spain and the United States regarded MacGregor and Aury as pirates.

Georges Biassou: Haitians in St. Augustine

In Haiti, black Haitian General Georges Biassou had allied with the Haitian leader Toussaint L'Ouverture. But when L'Ouverture accepted French promises of abolition of slavery and continued French control, Biassou and his forty-thousand-man army fought with the Spanish against the French. The Spanish provided Biassou's army with weapons, supplies, salaries, and Spanish citizenship. Biassou got a pension, a Spanish gold medal, and official thanks. The Spanish appointed him as a general of the "Black Auxiliaries of Carlos IV" in Santo Domingo.

Biassou moved with his family and a group of followers from Santo Domingo to St. Augustine in 1796. The Spanish East Florida

The Whetstone Chocolate Store occupies the Salcedo House that General Georges Biassou used as his home. Biassou commanded the Spanish-African militia in the 1790s.

governor appointed Biassou as leader of the Spanish-African militia, recognizing his experience as a leader and battle-hardened officer. The Black Spanish militia fought in several local wars, including the separatist rebellion of the so-called State of Muskogee, led by Loyalist William Augustus Bowles in 1800–1803, and engagements in the short Patriot War of 1812.

Biassou died in 1801, and the whole city, including the governor, turned out for his funeral. Although the location of Biassou's grave in the Tolomato Cemetery remains undetermined, Haitians still make pilgrimages to the grounds in his honor.

United States Eyes Florida: The Patriot War

George Matthews, a former American Revolutionary War officer, believed that Spanish rule would collapse in Florida with a slight push of military force. Amelia Island had become a thriving haven for smugglers, and the small Spanish garrison there appeared incapable of controlling the region. With support from President James Madison, Matthews and a small company of volunteers crossed into Spanish territory in March 1812, headed first for Amelia Island. Matthews lined up some support in Florida, including planter John McIntosh.

In this so-called Patriot War, the Georgians captured the town of Fernandina without a shot, outnumbering the Spanish garrison there two to one. They then marched south to the site of Fort Mose, where they encamped and demanded surrender of the capital city. The Spanish governor refused, knowing the fort and city walls could stave off the Georgians' paltry force of two hundred men. In Washington, President Madison cancelled support for the Patriot expedition; nevertheless, the invaders held on. The Spanish governor enlisted Seminoles and Afro-Seminoles to help fight the Patriots, who conducted raids as far south as present-day Flagler County, south of St. Augustine.

The Afro-Seminoles and Free Blacks

As Spanish control of East Florida waned, escaping African-American slaves fled from the United States to Florida. Some settled among free blacks in St. Augustine under the continuing sanctuary policy, while others joined with the Seminoles in areas where whites hadn't settled.

The Seminoles usually gave former slaves independent plots of land to work in exchange for a small token payment per year and the obligation to join in any skirmishes or battles with enemies. Although some intermarried with the Seminole people, the Afro-Seminoles tended to have separate village areas and farms, owing loyalty to a specific Seminole leader.

In the region around St. Augustine, Afro-Seminoles and free black men served as translators, working with Spanish authorities to resist the invasion by American Patriots in 1812. Governor Kindelán y Oregón relied on free black man Benjamin Wiggins and self-liberated slave Tony Proctor to enlist the support of the Seminoles under Chief Billy Bowlegs. Bowlegs agreed to send two hundred warriors to help the Spanish repel the Patriot invaders.

Florida Sold to the United States

With Spanish Florida troubled by invasions and local claims to sovereignty and with Spain's naval and land military stretched thin due to the revolutions sweeping South America, royal advisers decided that Spain could no longer hold Florida and St. Augustine. When the United States sent John Quincy Adams to negotiate a new boundary between the Spanish holdings in the New World and the United States, the Spanish proved more than agreeable. Giving up Florida seemed an entirely reasonable option.

In 1819 the Adams-Onis Treaty established the boundary between the U.S.-controlled Louisiana Purchase lands and Spanish territories farther west. That treaty also arranged the transfer of East and West Florida from Spain to the United States.

A formal ceremony in St. Augustine on July 10, 1821, marked the transfer of East Florida. Spanish troops and government officials departed for Cuba with their wives and children. Some one hundred slaves and free blacks, including the Biassou family, also left for Cuba.

The Seminoles and their black allies remained on their lands when the Spanish departed. They avoided the European-settled areas, living in scattered villages in Florida's interior. Conflicts between the U.S. government and the Seminoles would flare up in the coming years.

SITES TO SEE

City Gates

During the First Spanish, British, and Second Spanish Colonial Periods, city walls protected the city of St. Augustine, most notably the Cubo Wall, a reproduction of which stretches along the grounds of the Castillo de San Marcos.

The present-day City Gates at the intersection of Orange and St. George Streets—more properly referred to as the Guard Shelters—don't actually represent a gate in the ancient Cubo Line. Rather, Spanish authorities ordered the coquina towers in 1808 to replace wooden guardhouses originally built in 1739 in the Cubo Line. Captain Manuel de Hita designed the new towers. The Spanish first called the opening La Leche Gateway, as it led to the Mission Nombre de Dios with its Lady of La Leche shrine.

The two four-foot-square coquina pillars stand on each side of a twelve-foot-wide opening. Each of the towers measures fourteen feet high and was originally covered with white masonry trimmed with red plaster. A pomegranate carved from stone tops each tower. A symbol of resurrection and eternal life, the finial is appropriate for the long-lived city that survived so many attacks and fires.

The La Leche Gateway operated for decades, and the city's walls and gates protected its inhabitants from attack even after the United States took over, during the Second Seminole War. Situated at the north end of the pedestrian-only St. George Street, the guard towers are familiar landmarks.

Oldest Wooden Schoolhouse

Just a few yards from the guard towers of the City Gates, the old wooden schoolhouse at 14 St. George Street has been a Florida

Now reinforced with iron chains, the schoolhouse is one of the oldest wooden structures in the United States.

attraction for about a century. Constructed of termite-resistant red cedar and cypress, the building has survived Florida's harsh environment. Wooden pegs join the timbers, and handmade nails attach the siding. In 1937, when a hurricane threatened to destroy the structure, workers braced it with large iron chains to prevent the building from falling and to keep the leaning fireplace chimney on the outside kitchen from collapsing into the yard.

For a time, St. Augustinians promoted the building as the oldest frame house, but other structures in New England, New York, and

These animatronic figures greet visitors and talk about early classroom discipline and lessons in the oldest schoolhouse.

New Jersey predated it. In 1931 locals modified the claim to the oldest wooden schoolhouse, a term more historically accurate.

Greek/Minorcan Ioannis Giannopoulous owned the building in its early years and was the school's original teacher. He later Hispanicized his name to Juan Genopoly or Janopoli. He survived his first three wives, and his fourth bore three children. They lived upstairs and did quite well on the proceeds from the pupils' tuition. Records suggest he taught both boys and girls as early as 1788.

Animatronic figures dressed to represent a late eighteenth-century teacher and pupils greet you in the oldest schoolhouse. The mannequins tell the story of the classroom and the lessons. Books, slates, a dunce hat, and several cooking utensils of the era are on display. The backyard contains a pecan tree that has been dated at more than 250 years old, as well as a replica of the outdoor toilet, or privy.

Cathedral

During the British occupation, St. Augustine's Catholic churches stood abandoned and partially destroyed. When the Spanish returned in the 1780s, Catholicism was revived. At the urging of Father Hassett, one of the priests who ministered to the growing Catholic community, Spanish government officials authorized work on a Catholic parish church on February 13, 1788. The Spanish Crown approved the plans for the church in 1790.

Work on the church began in 1793. Don Miguel Ysnardy served as architect and later as steward of the building. In order to get material for the structure and to honor earlier religious buildings, workers collected coquina from the previous mission and parish churches. The church held its dedication services on December 8, 1797.

On April 12, 1887, a fire began in the nearby St. Augustine Hotel. It spread to the church, destroying part of the structure. Bishop John Moore, Bishop Verot's successor, appealed for funds to rebuild. The current Cathedral represents a much later reconstruction on the grounds of the original parish church.

As work progressed, builders expanded the structure with transepts and a new bell tower, creating the present Spanish Mission Revival–style facade. In the 1960s, Archbishop Joseph P. Hurley, the sixth bishop of St. Augustine, commissioned yet another renovation of the Cathedral, adding the historic interior murals representing the First Mass at Seloy. On March 9, 1966, William Cardinal Conway, Archbishop of Armagh in Ireland, presided over the opening and dedication services. On December 4, 1976, Pope Paul VI designated the Cathedral a minor basilica.

Plaza de la Constitución Monument

In the plaza, directly across from the entrance to the Cathedral, a monument reflects the official Spanish name of the plaza and recognizes the Spanish Constitution of 1812. The story of the obelisk and the naming of the square reflect the broader history of Spain and the Spanish Empire during this era.

Meeting in the city of Cádiz, the *Cortes Generales,* or Spanish national assembly, promulgated a new constitution on March 19, 1812. The *Cortes* produced an extraordinarily modern constitution for the period that guaranteed universal male suffrage, national

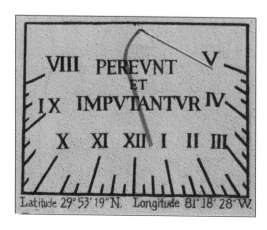

This vertical sundial on the wall of the Cathedral is a perfect way to check your watch for accuracy. It is set for Eastern Standard Time at this latitude and longitude.

The Spanish Constitution of 1812 declared democratic principles. Local Spanish liberals restored the inscription on the base of this monument after conservative authorities had it removed.

sovereignty, freedom of the press, and land reform.

In 1812 the liberal *Cortes* ordered that all plazas in the Spanish empire be renamed and dedicated to the new constitution and its liberal principles. Here and there across Spanish America, local authorities complied and erected monuments. But as soon as Ferdinand VII assumed power, he annulled the liberals' order. Officials in Havana renamed the plaza once again and, throughout the empire, monuments disappeared one by one. But in St. Augustine, liberal sentiment prevailed and the plaza retained its name. Conservative authorities in Cuba ordered the St. Augustine plaque removed. Local Spanish liberals restored the plaque just at the end of the Second Spanish Period (1819–1820). When the Americans took over in 1821, they left the plaque and the name in place.

Military Hospital Museum

Across the plaza, on the south side, stands the arched entrance to Aviles Street, so named for the birthplace of Admiral Menéndez. Until 1923, maps showed the street as Hospital Street, named for the

The Military Hospital Museum is a favorite stop on school and visitor tours and contains artifacts representing Colonial-era medical practices. More than fifteen thousand children tour the museum each year.

Royal Hospital of Our Lady of Guadalupe a few doors down.

The Spanish Military Hospital at 3 Aviles Street is in an entirely reconstructed building, representing the hospital that operated on the site during the Second Spanish Period. The museum speaks not only to the history of St. Augustine but also to general medical history since 1791. Docent-led tours highlight the medical paraphernalia collected in each room. The Mourning Room contains the various items used by Catholic priests to perform last rites for patients about to die. The Surgeon's Office includes surgical tools, some of which are still used today. The Ward Room is a replica of a hospital room of the period. Since so many patients suffered from dysentery, the cots have an appropriate section cut away and bedpans underneath. The Apothecary Office displays the equipment used to prepare medicines in the 1790s.

Don Manuel Solana House

The Don Manuel Solana House is located at 21 Aviles Street and is now the Casa de Solana Bed and Breakfast Inn. Don Manuel Solana built the house after 1788, and the building later became the home of Oliver Bronson Jr., a county commissioner after the Civil War. The house reflects the coquina architecture of the Second Spanish Period and features a loggia, or covered patio, visible from the gates on Aviles Street.

Parts of the house date back to Don Manuel Lorenzo Solana, born in St. Augustine on April 7, 1740, of parents who were also natives of the city. When most of the Spanish left Florida in 1764 at the beginning of the British Period, Solana remained. He married an English girl, Mary Mitchell, and had at least two children with her. They later separated, and he married Mary Mestre, a Minorcan, with whom he fathered several more children. When the Spanish returned, Solana acquired title to the land and to some other property previously owned by the Solana family. By 1793 Solana lived at this

The Don Manuel Solana House is now the Casa de Solana Bed and Breakfast Inn.

site with children from both his first and second marriages. He developed a reputation for treating Seminoles who came into town kindly and offering them protection.

Records suggest that sometime between 1803 and 1820 Solana

Seminole

The name for the Native American people who settled in Florida from the late 1700s into the early 1800s was Seminole. The word *seminole* probably has its origin in the Spanish word *cimarron,* meaning wild or runaway. The original Timucua, Calusa, and other tribes had virtually become extinct under Spanish rule, and the Seminoles were in fact refugees from other groups to the north, primarily the Creek and Miccosukee peoples of Georgia and Alabama. The Seminoles had escaped conflicts among tribes in Alabama and Georgia.

built the original house that is now part of the Casa de Solana Bed and Breakfast Inn. Some features of the original construction remain, including the coquina blocks, pegged ceiling beams, and an exterior balcony. One of the walls around the property and the enclosed courtyard dates from the earlier English period. Solana, who also owned a plantation out of town, died in 1821. Since he left behind a large number of children, the name Solana became common among later generations of St. Augustinians.

Father Miguel O'Reilly House

The O'Reilly House at 32 Aviles Street, like the home and chapel of Father Camps, represents the effort to reestablish a Catholic

Builders laid the original foundation of the O'Reilly House in the seventeenth century. In the 1790s, Father Miguel O'Reilly established a home and school here.

presence in St. Augustine after the departure of the British in 1784. The building itself, one of the oldest in the city, has walls dating to around 1691.

Father Miguel O'Reilly arrived in St. Augustine in 1785 to serve as parish priest. His house also served as a school, where he tutored numerous young Catholics, including Felix Varela, who spent his childhood in St. Augustine. Varela moved on to school in Havana and to a distinguished career in the mid-1800s as a defender of Irish immigrants to New York City. Cuba honors him as an advocate of Cuban independence from Spain.

The Sisters of St. Joseph have served as guardians and operators of the building since their arrival in St. Augustine from France in 1866. The sisters lived upstairs and taught school on the first floor. Their curriculum included specialized arts and crafts such as lace-making, tapestry painting, and china painting. In the 1940s, they ordered the ground floor tiled, new cypress ceilings installed on the first and second floors, and the fireplaces restored.

You can see the details of the house's construction by viewing a section of exposed wall showing both the tabby (rough cement with oyster shells) and the coquina block. The Menéndez Room contains displays on the founding of the city, as well as information about the Cathedral and the first parish church in the United States. The St. Augustine Room contains numerous artifacts, including a printing press made in 1889. The press printed the school's monthly newspaper, *Pascua Florida,* from 1889 to 1909. There's also a ten-minute video that details the history of the house.

Chapter 5
TERRITORIAL AND EARLY
STATEHOOD PERIOD, 1821–1861

Under U.S. control in 1821, West and East Florida united into one territory with two capitals, Pensacola and St. Augustine. However, having two capital cities proved unworkable when the Florida Territorial Council had to travel between the two. Governor William Pope Duval appointed a commission to decide on a suitable location for a new territorial capital. The commission designated a spot at the old Apalachee mission center at San Luis. In 1824 Florida established Tallahassee as its new capital. It was roughly halfway between St. Augustine and Pensacola, about two hundred miles from each. No longer a capital city, St. Augustine suddenly became a minor local administrative and commercial center.

Yet, during the next forty years, the city found a new identity as a tourist destination for Americans from the North. As St. Augustinians adapted to the American way of life, they developed new institutions,

---

William Pope Duval

Under the state constitution of Florida, a governor may serve only one four-year term (or a maximum of six years if he or she is finishing the term of a prior governor). However, one Florida governor served twelve years.

In the period 1821–1845, Florida was a U.S. territory and its governors were appointed by the president of the United States. President James Monroe named North Carolina native William Pope Duval a United States judge for the East Florida district on May 18, 1821. A year later, Monroe appointed Duval as the first non-military governor of the territory, following a one-year term by General Andrew Jackson. Duval was reappointed by John Quincy Adams and Andrew Jackson. Following retirement from the governorship in 1834, Duval practiced law in Florida before moving to Texas in 1848.

In the 1820s, impressed by scenes like this on Marine Street, American visitors started calling St. Augustine the Ancient City. The architecture and exotic Spanish history appealed to the Romantic sensitivities of the era.

including Christian churches, schools, boardinghouses, inns, and hotels. Newspapers, wholesale businesses, and shipping lines tied the city to the rest of the nation. The American settlers and local officials established cemeteries, constructed new public buildings, and made civic improvements.

Rather than viewing the crumbling remains of past eras and the alleylike dirt streets as simply decrepit, newcomers and visitors found the city's antiquity and its exotic inhabitants charming. Between 1821 and 1861, writers and artists highlighted the Romantic viewpoint. For the Romantic sensibility, St. Augustine had great appeal, with its narrow streets, unique architecture, castlelike fort, Greek and Spanish heritage, and dark legends of massacres, pirate raids, and sieges.

In addition to its Romantic appeal, the city drew visitors because of its climate. Winters in St. Augustine felt so much milder than in any other city on the East Coast. "Invalids" came as the first tourists. They wrote letters home and sometimes published their accounts, reflecting their impressions. Most of them commented on the city's hospitality and antiquity as well as its warm weather.

Ancient City

The term ancient city in reference to St. Augustine first cropped up in the 1820s. Episcopal Reverend R.A. Henderson used the expression in print when he reported from St. Augustine in the *Philadelphia Recorder* on March 21, 1829. He found "comparative comfort in one of the few rooms to be found in this ancient city, furnished with the modern luxuries of a chimney and glass windows." Other letter writers, essayists, and travelers would continue to use the expression throughout the years, establishing it as the unofficial nickname of St. Augustine. It became more official between 1850 and 1854 with the publication of the newspaper *The Ancient City*.

Seminole War

Despite the burst of development and new settlers, nearby farms and plantations suddenly became unsafe during the Second Seminole War (1835–1842). St. Augustine remained a place of refuge for plantation families, and several enterprising families were added to the town's population.

The Second Seminole War grew out of the national Indian Removal Policy enacted under President Andrew Jackson in 1830. The policy required the removal of Native Americans from Georgia, Alabama, Mississippi, and Florida to reservation lands in Indian

Seminole Wars

Three Seminole Wars were fought between U.S. army forces and the Seminoles. St. Augustine provided a refuge for planters and others displaced by the wars.

First Seminole War, 1817–18: Andrew Jackson sided with the White Stick Creek Indians against the Red Stick Creek Indians, driving the latter as fugitives into Florida as he invaded northwest Florida. The Red Sticks became one of the major groups forming the Seminoles.

Second Seminole War, 1835–42: Seminoles under the leadership of Osceola, Micanopy, and others resisted the Indian Removal order to deport them west to Indian Territory (Oklahoma).

Third Seminole War or Billy Bowlegs' War, 1855–58: This was an uprising of bands of Seminoles who had refused deportation and had retreated southward. No peace treaty was ever signed, and the Seminoles in Florida long claimed to represent the one Native American group that never surrendered to the United States.

Territory, which later became the state of Oklahoma. Jackson and his followers believed that Native Americans and their black allies had no right to occupy the rich, potential plantation lands of the Southeast.

Some of the Seminoles, under the leadership of Osceola, King Philip, and Micanopy, refused to go peacefully to the resettlement area in the West. They couldn't get guarantees of land in the Indian Territory independent of their traditional enemies, the Creeks, nor could they be assured that the African Seminoles among them would remain free. The Seminole leaders who opposed removal to the West opted for war.

St. Augustine's Joseph Marion Hernandez served as a brigadier general of Florida volunteers in the war against the Seminoles. In 1837, as Seminole resistance continued, Hernandez captured King

Philip and rounded up others. From captivity, Philip sent a message to his son Coacoochee, asking that he come see him. Coacoochee arrived under a white plume, a symbol of truce, but Hernandez took him and his followers into custody. When Osceola came under a similar flag of truce, Hernandez, following orders from U.S. Army General Thomas S. Jesup, also arrested Osceola. The arrests of the leaders didn't end the war, however.

The Army held the Seminole prisoners in the bombproof rooms at Fort Marion. In a daring nighttime escape on November 28, 1837, twenty of them fled. Osceola, suffering from malaria, couldn't join them. After the escape, the Army transferred Osceola to Fort Moultrie in Charleston, South Carolina. He died there on January 21, 1838.

Boardinghouses and Hotels

A number of women emerged as successful entrepreneurs and managers of boardinghouses and inns during this period, known locally as the Boardinghouse Era. At least three of them had been planters' wives or daughters, and no doubt their experience in managing domestic servants, handling large household budgets, and arranging hospitality for visitors carried over to their boardinghouse managerial tasks. These enterprising women left behind physical imprints of their lives and careers in several structures still standing in the city, such as the St. Francis Inn and the Ximenez-Fatio House.

Steamboats

The steamboat era defined the transportation history of the southern United States from the 1820s through the 1870s. Before rail lines penetrated much of Florida, steamboats plied the rivers and coast, providing the best way to reach St. Augustine.

Some Northern tourists traveled by train to Savannah, Georgia, then took steamboats by way of the Atlantic and the St. Johns River to Jacksonville. From there, they steamed south on the river to a transfer point at Picolata. There they off-loaded their luggage and boarded a stagecoach for the short but sometimes rugged eighteen-mile overland trip to St. Augustine. Today County Road 208 follows the old carriage route.

From the 1840s, the Savannah Line ran steamers from Savannah that stopped at Jacksonville, Picolata, and Palatka. Advertisements for the line ran in the *New York Daily Times* throughout the 1850s, stressing the regularly scheduled runs of three steamboats and accommodations for invalids.

SITES TO SEE

A New Cemetery

In its first decade under American control, the city struggled through a yellow fever epidemic. The town council established a cemetery to accommodate the many who died: the Old Presbyterian Cemetery, also known as the Huguenot Cemetery. Few, if any, French Huguenots lived in St. Augustine during this period, so it appears that the name reflected the Spanish St. Augustinian heritage that regarded all Protestants as Huguenots. This harks back to the first conflict between Spanish St. Augustine and the French from Fort Caroline and to the slaughter of Huguenots at Matanzas.

Yellow fever struck the city just as the United States took over Florida in 1821. With so many fatalities, Protestant Americans established the Huguenot Cemetery just north of the City Gates at the end of St. George Street.

Castillo de San Marcos/Fort Marion Improvements

During the Territorial Period, U.S. troops occupied Castillo de San Marcos. However, the fort fell into partial decay, as troops didn't regularly stay there or use it as a fortification. The gates remained open, even at night. Visitors remarked on the semi-abandoned fort, with owls roosting in the corner towers, already a regular part of the Ancient City's attractions.

In the years from 1835 to 1842, the Army Corps of Engineers rebuilt and lowered the seawall at the Castillo with embrasures for new cannons placed just above sea level. This so-called water battery could fire straight at approaching enemy vessels. Behind the water battery, the Army built a "hot shot" oven to heat cannonballs so they might ignite enemy ships' sails or hulls or penetrate and detonate their powder magazines. You can still see the semicircular gun mounts for the water battery guns, but workers filled the firing gaps in the seawall with stone.

Inside the fort, workers converted several of the casemate rooms to prison cells, often referred to incorrectly as dungeons. These cells held Chief Horse, Osceola, Wild Cat, and other Seminole captives.

St. Augustine Seawall

The seawall along the Matanzas River waterfront of St. Augustine was repaired in 2011, after the city spent considerable effort searching for funds to protect the downtown from flooding and water damage. The wall had been reconstructed in the 1830s from an earlier, Spanish-era coquina wall.

In 1832 more than one hundred local citizens signed a petition asking Congress to appropriate funds for the wall that reached from "the fort and stretching along in front of the city." They asked to rebuild "the remains of a sea wall which was found necessary to protect it from the violence of the equinoctial storms." The petitioners also pointed out that "a considerable portion of this wall was improvidently taken away to construct a wharf in front of the Barrack for the use of the United States' troops, leaving much property both public and private exposed to inevitable ruin," with houses being "destroyed and whole lots overflowed." The Army Corps of Engineers, with the help of slaves rented from local owners, rebuilt the seawall in 1833, extending it south of the plaza. Lt. Francis L. Dancy supervised work on portions of the wall that are still standing. Today street signs warn visitors that high tides and storm water still can flood cars parked on Avenida Menendez just a few blocks south of the plaza.

The 1832 petitioners also asked for improvements to the Castillo, noting that it "afforded ample protection to the city during the time of the Spanish sway and is now rapidly dilapidating and passing into ruin." In another petition in 1834, the citizens remarked on both the practical and historical significance of the fort: "It is desirous that

Along the waterfront on Avenida Menendez, this seawall partially protects the residences across the street from high winds and tides.

it may be preserved in its primitive condition for the purposes of continuing an ancient fort which will for centuries be useful as a monument of Spanish operations." The massive fortress had already become a historical attraction.

St. Augustine National Cemetery

St. Augustine National Cemetery occupies a small plot on Marine Street just south of the St. Francis Barracks. Authorities designated this burial ground as a national cemetery in 1881, but the graveyard was established much earlier, during the Territorial Period. Soldiers who died while stationed with the U.S. Army in St. Augustine were buried there beginning in 1828. It was greatly expanded during and after the Second Seminole War, beginning with the slaughter of Major Francis Dade's forces on their march from Tampa to Fort King

(Ocala), near present-day Bushnell, in December 1835.

When U.S. troops finally reached the site of the Dade Battlefield a month later, they found only the skeletons of the dead. Troops hastily buried the remains on the spot. In 1842, after the end of the war, the Army decided to remove the bodies of all U.S. troops who had been killed in the war, including those in Dade's command, to a single burial site.

The Army interred the remains of 1,468 soldiers in collective crypts at the cemetery. To mark those interments, the Army erected

Beneath these unusual coquina pyramids are the remains of more than fourteen hundred U.S. troops killed in the Second Seminole War. The obelisk was added in 1881 to memorialize the dead.

This 1938 superintendent's cottage at the National Cemetery matches local styles and construction methods of the pre–Civil War period.

three unusual coquina pyramids, which still stand. Nearby, plain markers indicate the graves of Seminole Indian scouts who worked with the Army. A formal ceremony dedicated the pyramids on August 14, 1842.

As part of the upgrade of the cemetery, the Army erected a monument in 1881 to the soldiers who died in the Florida wars. Known as the Dade Monument, it is a tall marble and coquina obelisk that stands in front of the three pyramids. Soldiers at the St. Francis Barracks donated one day's pay to help fund the memorial. A coquina wall built at the same time still encloses the cemetery. The Army acquired additional land in 1912 and 1913, increasing the site to 1.36 acres.

The city council approved the design of a new superintendent's cottage in 1938 in an effort to have it conform to the local architectural heritage. The design used coquina and featured an overhanging balcony and shingle roof. At the same time, builders added a coquina rostrum at the northern end of the cemetery to serve as a setting for ceremonies. It too echoed the Spanish style found throughout the city.

The Fernandez-Llambias House

Like several other historic homes in St. Augustine with long histories, the Fernandez-Llambias House at 31 St. Francis Street is named after two owners from different periods. The building is located a few yards from the Oldest House complex and the Tovar House. The original date of construction isn't known, but the house was owned by Pedro Fernandez in 1763. Originally a single-story coquina house, it had a concrete floor made of oyster shells, sand, and lime. The building changed hands several times during the British Period, and later owners enlarged it with the addition of a two-room second story accessible only by an outside staircase. Dona Catalina Llambias bought the home in 1854, and it remained in the Llambias family for sixty-five years.

The Carnegie Institution of Washington, aided by the St. Augustine Historical Society, bought the Llambias House in 1938 and then deeded it in trust to the city. In 1954 the St. Augustine Restoration and Preservation Association restored the building under the direction of architect Stuart Barnette. The Altrusa Club became custodian of the property in 1967. In 1970 the house was designated a national historic landmark. The St. Augustine Historical Society purchased the adjoining corner lot in 1973 so that the architectural integrity of the building and neighborhood could be preserved. The present appearance of the building reflects the Territorial Period of 1821 to 1845.

The eighteenth-century Fernandez-Llambias House is one block from the back of the St. Francis Barracks. The wooden second story with balcony atop a coquina first floor was a common local feature. The house has been restored to its appearance during the period before the Civil War.

St. Francis Inn

Completed in the 1790s, the St. Francis Inn dates to the Second Spanish Period but is also part of the Boardinghouse Era. During the Second Spanish Period, Gaspar Garcia, a sergeant in the Spanish force stationed in St. Augustine, lived in the home. In 1802 sea captain Juan Ruggiers bought the house. By 1838 retired Royal Marine Colonel Thomas Henry Dummett owned the building.

Although T. H. Dummett and his wife, Mary, had eleven children, only a few lived to adulthood. Dummett had moved to Florida from either Barbados or the Bahamas, and he bought a sugar plantation and mill on the Tomoka River, south of St. Augustine. Ruins of the sugar mill and a rum-processing facility can still be seen near Titusville, just off the Old Dixie Highway, north of Ormond. A historic marker identifies the spot.

The St. Francis Inn has operated under various names for more than one and a half centuries. An artesian well in the courtyard feeds into a fishpond.

The family evacuated the plantation during the Second Seminole War and, like other families, took shelter in St. Augustine. In 1845 Anna Dummett, one of the colonel's daughters, converted their town house into an inn. Like several other inns run by plantation refugee women, the St. Francis Inn did extremely well and developed a reputation for elegant hospitality. Although she never gave up her British citizenship, Anna Dummett would later become a dedicated advocate of the Confederate cause. Until her death in 1899 at age eighty, she remained a leader in St. Augustine among those preserving the memory of Florida's role in the Confederacy. In 1888 John L. Wilson purchased the inn and made several renovations and additions.

In later eras, numerous writers famous in their day stayed in the inn, including Pulitzer Prize winners Van Wycks Brooks, author of *The Flowering of New England* (1936), and Gladys Hasty Caroll, author of *As the Earth Turns* (1933). Over the years, the St. Francis Inn's name changed a number of times. A full list is available at the front desk.

Prince Murat House

Although built during the Second Spanish Period, the Prince Murat house is maintained to represent the early Territorial Period, when its most famous owner occupied it. The house is located in the Dow

From the 1930s through the 1950s, Kenneth Worcester Dow collected eight historic homes and moved them to lots surrounding the Prince Murat House. They are now managed by the Museum of Arts & Sciences of Daytona Beach.

This bust of Napoleon Bonaparte inside the Murat House looks a lot like Prince Murat, who lived here in the 1820s.

Museum/Old St. Augustine Village at 250 Cordova Street. Prince of Naples Achille Murat, a nephew of Napoleon Bonaparte, boarded at the house for several months in 1824, and it is probably in this home that he entertained Ralph Waldo Emerson. A known freethinker and a supposed staunch defender of slavery, he joined the local Masonic lodge.

The Canova family owned the house and most of the block from 1821 until well after the Civil War. Murat probably lived in the house for only less than a year before moving to Tallahassee and may have returned from time to time later in the 1830s. To memorialize

---

Dow Museum

The Dow Museum of Historic Houses, located at 149 Cordova Street, is a collection of nine homes that was established by avid antiques collector Kenneth Worcester Dow. He donated the house collection to St. Augustine in 1989, to be administered by the Museum of Arts & Sciences of Daytona Beach. Opened in the 2000, the collection includes the following homes:

1. The Star General Store was built by merchant Emanuel de Medici in 1899.

2. Kenneth Dow started the collection with the purchase of the Prince Murat house in 1940.

3. The Dow House was built by Antonio Canova in 1839. Kenneth Dow bought it in 1941.

4. Canova House is the third oldest house on the property, built by Antonio Canova in 1840.

5. The Worcester House was built on the property in 1906 and is named for Dow's aunt, who lived there.

6. The Carpenter's House was built from leftover materials from the Worcester and Spear Houses.

7. Constructed in 1903, the Spear House often features works of local artists.

8. The Howells House was a winter rental built in 1907 and is named for William Dean Howells, who wintered there in 1916.

9. The Rose House is named for author and rose collector Jean Wickham Reilly, who rented the house from 1956 to 1966.

---

his stay, the house is decorated with Empire-style furniture and sculptures and artifacts echoing Murat's tenure there.

Murat served as an officer in the Florida Militia and briefly returned to Europe, where he served as a colonel in the Belgian Legion. The fact that Murat resembled his uncle in appearance and some mannerisms may have contributed to his decision not to resettle in Europe, where the older regimes feared the rise of another

Napoleon throughout the 1830s.

In later life, after moving to Tallahassee, Murat practiced law and became mayor of the city. He married Catherine Dangerfield Willis Gray, a great-grandniece of George Washington.

The Dow Museum includes eight other homes from various periods of St. Augustine's long history that have been built on the grounds. A display inside the visitors center explains the Kenneth Dow endowment and house collection and also contains a diorama of the city during the First Spanish Period.

Ximenez-Fatio House

One of the most authentic historic properties in the city and located on the corner of Cadiz and Aviles Streets, the Ximenez-Fatio House is maintained as a museum. The site includes a coquina house, as

The Colonial Dames of America administer the Ximenez-Fatio House, a carefully restored example of the Boardinghouse Era in St. Augustine.

Ponce de León, who first discovered Florida in 1513, overlooks the plaza and harbor at St. Augustine.

Early visitors to Florida and St. Augustine reported wildlife like this blue heron, performing his dance in the shallow waters of St. Augustine harbor.

Ivan Mestrovic sculpted the statue of Father Francisco Lopez de Mendoza Grajales that stands in line with the tall cross at the Mission Nombre de Dios.

At the Cathedral, this mural by Hugo Ohlms depicts the first Mass ever celebrated in St. Augustine.

The reconstructed rustic altar at the waterfront matches the depiction in the mural by Hugo Ohlms.

This massive, seventeenth-century fort is St. Augustine's premier visitor attraction.

From the upper walls, you can look down on the bombproof rooms of the Castillo de San Marcos that harbored city residents during attacks and bombardments by the British.

These guard towers at the north end of St. George Street, known as the City Gates, served as the north entry through the wall that surrounded the city.

This bastion tower overlooks the marshes of Matanzas Inlet.

Guns like these protected the waterway approach to St. Augustine from the south.

St. Photios, the patron saint of the Greek Catholic Church, is on display at the St. Photios Shrine on St. George Street. The shrine and museum commemorate the Greeks and Minorcans who fled from an exploitative plantation in New Smyrna to St. Augustine in 1777.

Dr. Andrew Anderson renovated Markland House, now part of Flagler College. Anderson, a civic leader from the 1880s through the 1920s, made many contributions to memorialize the city's history.

The Casa Monica Hotel, restored and modernized, recalls the Gilded Age luxury established by Franklin Smith and Henry Flagler.

The St. Augustine Lighthouse, built in 1874, overlooks the city, harbor, and ocean, providing a spectacular view for those who climb the 165-foot-tall tower.

This fanciful little castle, modeled in part on the Alhambra in Spain, helped bring Moorish Revival architecture to Florida and the United States.

Flagler College now occupies the former Ponce de Leon Hotel. The building and grounds are kept in excellent condition.

These lifelike figures greet visitors at the Old City Jail.

Henry Flagler needed the land owned by the Methodist Church in order to build the Alcazar, so he financed this Spanish Renaissance Revival church several blocks away in return for the center city lot he wanted.

Flagler had this church built in less than a year to honor the memory of his daughter, Jenny Louise Benedict. Modeled after St. Mark's Basilica in Venice, it is a rare example of Italian Renaissance Revival architecture in the United States.

Both the Lightner Museum and several city of St. Augustine offices now occupy this building, originally the Alcazar Hotel.

The fourth floor added to house extra guests in the original Alcazar Hotel now overlooks the inner courtyard of the Lightner Museum.

This birdhouse is an exact scale model of the Generals' House and stands in its front yard.

The Bridge of Lions, recently rebuilt and upgraded, connects St. Augustine to Anastasia Island.

The Bridge of Lions drawbridge stands open while sailboats anchor out in the harbor.

Sculpted by Raffaello Romanelli, donated by Dr. Andrew Anderson, and refurbished by Enzo Torcoletti, this is one of two lions that guard the Bridge of Lions.

The Black Raven Pirate Ship, moored near the Bridge of Lions, welcomes guests seeking to find their "inner pirate."

Ripley's Believe It or Not Museum occupies three stories inside the crenellated walls of the Warden Castle.

Johnny Depp is honored in wax at Potter's Wax Museum, where changing displays keep pace with popular culture depictions of piracy.

At Marineland, the first oceanarium in the world, the dolphins are friendly and curious.

well as two detached buildings: a kitchen and a washhouse. Andres Ximenez built the house in 1798. He operated a general store, billiard room, and tavern on the first floor and housed his large family upstairs.

Despite its original construction, it has been restored to represent the Boardinghouse Era during the U.S. Territorial and Early Statehood Period. Margaret Cook, who had moved to St. Augustine from South Carolina in 1821, purchased the building after her husband's death in 1826. She hired (or went into partnership with) Eliza Whitehurst, who operated the house as a boardinghouse until her death in 1839.

Sarah Anderson bought the building from Mrs. Cook in 1838. Mrs. Anderson had owned Dunlawton Plantation, which was destroyed in 1836 during the Second Seminole War. She moved into the house with her extended family to be safe in the city during the remainder of the war. In 1855 Mrs. Anderson asked her friend Louisa Fatio to manage the building as a boardinghouse. Louisa Fatio had fled from New Switzerland, a plantation established by her grandfather Francis Philip Fatio and was destroyed during the Patriot War of 1812. The rebuilt Fatio plantation was again destroyed during the Second Seminole War.

Louisa Fatio bought the boardinghouse from Mrs. Anderson in 1855 and continued to run it. She had a reputation for excellent service and fine cuisine that spread among visitors.

In 1939 the Society of Florida Colonial Dames purchased the house from Judge David Dunham, a nephew of Louisa Fatio. The society has operated it as a historical museum since 1946. The house is furnished with authentic, pre–Civil War–era furniture, decorative items, and linens. Each room is decorated with a different theme in mind. The Captain's Room, for example, contains artifacts that would relate to the life of a visiting sea captain.

The Segui/Kirby Smith House

On Aviles Street next to the Ximenez-Fatio House, the Segui/Kirby Smith House also traces its history to before the Territorial and Early Statehood Period. Bernardo Segui bought the building in 1786. When Judge Joseph Lee Smith arrived in St. Augustine in 1821, he rented the house and then purchased it a few years later. His son, the future Confederate General Edmund Kirby Smith, was born in the house in 1824. During the Civil War, General Kirby Smith became commander of Confederate forces west of the Mississippi.

Alexander Darnes, a family slave sixteen years younger than Edmund Kirby Smith, accompanied the general as his valet during the war. After the war, Darnes attended secondary school and then

Inside the courtyard of the Segui/Kirby Smith House stand statues representing Dr. Alexander Darnes (left) and Confederate General Edmund Kirby Smith.

Howard Medical School, from which he received his medical degree in 1880, becoming the first black physician in Florida. Dr. Darnes practiced medicine in St. Augustine for the next fourteen years. When he died in 1894, three thousand people attended his funeral.

In 1895 John and Elizabeth Wilson donated the house to the St. Augustine Free Public Library Association, as noted in an inscription over the front door. It remains the property of the library. In 1995 the St. Augustine Historical Society moved its research library to the location, which now houses thousands of books, photos, maps, and archival manuscript collections available to researchers and the public.

In 1997 the Florida legislature established a program to commemorate individuals selected as great Floridians. Edmund Kirby Smith and Dr. Alexander Darnes both earned the honor. Maria Kirby Smith, the great-granddaughter of the general, sculpted the statues of Dr. Darnes and General Kirby Smith that now stand in the courtyard of the Segui/Kirby Smith House. Kirby Smith is depicted in his senior years, when he was the chancellor of the University of Nashville and a professor of mathematics at the University of the South at Sewanee.

Trinity Episcopal Church

Located on the Plaza de la Constitución with an entrance at 5 Artillery Lane, Trinity Episcopal Church has a long history. The Trinity Parish of the Episcopal Church in St. Augustine was established in 1821 and can rightfully claim to be the oldest Protestant congregation in Florida. Construction of the first church building, made of coquina, began in 1830. The congregation first met for services in 1831 in the tiny structure, which measured only thirty-six by fifty feet.

The original building survived the Territorial and Early Statehood Period with minor improvements, including three stained glass windows added just before the Civil War. Perhaps spurred

The St. Augustine Episcopal congregation traces its origins to 1821 and is the oldest Protestant congregation in Florida. The 1830s Trinity Episcopal Church faces the plaza, directly across from the Catholic Cathedral.

by Henry Flagler's funding of new Methodist and Presbyterian structures, the Reverend C.M. Sturges began a six-year fund-raising effort to remodel the building. The church reopened in 1903 with the present neo-Gothic style of architecture. Other additions in the 1950s and 1960s included a two-story education area, a new parish hall, and a new organ.

Chapter 6
THE CIVIL WAR AND THE GILDED AGE, 1861–1913

During the Civil War, Confederate forces briefly controlled St. Augustine; later, the U.S. Army occupied and governed the city. Following the war, African-Americans established Lincolnville, a neighborhood on the western edge of the city. St. Augustine resumed its role as a destination for visitors, and several Northern millionaires built winter homes there. Henry Flagler and others built elegant hotels, seeking to attract more affluent visitors.

The Gilded Age

By the 1870s and 1880s, St. Augustine had become even more accessible to Northern visitors than during the pre–Civil War years. In 1867 the first telegraph line reached the city. Steamboats still plied the St. Johns River from Jacksonville, with stops at Picolata and East Palatka, points linked by stagecoach over improved roads into St. Augustine. A narrow-gauge railroad line from Jacksonville to St. Augustine that had been destroyed during the Civil War reopened in the early 1880s. Northern tourists could travel by rail or steamer to Jacksonville, then continue to St. Augustine by train.

By the 1880s, the style of tourism in St. Augustine changed from isolated visits of "invalids" to a steady trickle of affluent visitors. During the Gilded Age, many wealthy Northerners invested in private winter homes in the city, including Bostonian Franklin W. Smith, who made his fortune in hardware, and William G. Warden, a business partner of John D. Rockefeller.

Henry Flagler, the financial mastermind behind Standard Oil, visited St. Augustine and developed a passion for it, deciding to invest in new hotels and other real estate in and around the city. He made so many spectacular and long-lasting contributions to the

---

Flagler Versus Plant

Henry Flagler's rival in Florida rail and hotel expansion was Henry J. Plant (1819–1899), who consolidated several rail lines and built new ones throughout Florida. While Plant's lines ran to the Gulf Coast, Flager's ran south from St. Augustine on the Atlantic Coast. In 1891 Plant opened the lavish, Moorish-style Tampa Bay Hotel. Like the competing Ponce de Leon Hotel built by Flagler in St. Augustine, the Tampa Bay Hotel later became part of a college campus.

---

city's development that St. Augustine remembers the period from the late 1880s through about 1900 as the Flagler Era.

Flagler envisioned St. Augustine as a "winter Newport" where the wealthy could enjoy Florida's balmy climate in suitable accommodations. Newport, Rhode Island, developed as a summer resort because its location on a peninsula provided cooling cross-breezes throughout the hot months. Dozens of millionaires from all over the Northeast built homes there, and Flagler envisioned a similar boom for St. Augustine as a winter destination.

The Gilded Age ushered in an era of conspicuous consumption in the United States, and Flagler's St. Augustine hotels thrived because of it. Flagler's hotels welcomed wealthy and famous visitors, and the resultant publicity of their trips brought even more travelers. Less affluent tourists arrived to watch the elegantly attired millionaires shop in expensive boutiques inside the hotel complexes and take hired carriage and oxcart rides around the city's landmarks.

Flagler and Civic Improvements

Flagler's impact on St. Augustine went far beyond his construction of two hotels and purchase of a third. To support his guests' comfort,

Taken from the Ponce de Leon Hotel in the 1890s, this photo shows the Cordova (Casa Monica) to the left of the Alcazar in the background across the park. The horse-drawn taxis stood ready to take guests on a tour. (Courtesy of the Library of Congress)

Flagler had water supplies and sewer lines built and encouraged city residents to tie in to the new lines. He purchased the railroad from Jacksonville in 1885 and renovated and improved the St. Augustine railroad station. He had the line converted from narrow gauge to standard in 1890. Telephones came in 1888, and in the same year the Ponce de Leon lit up with electric lights. It was the first building in the state of Florida to have electricity.

Flagler built a local hospital in 1890 named Alicia after his second wife, Alice, and a new city jail in 1891 known as the Old City Jail. The building's name led to a bit of confusion: The city was old but not the jail. He funded a new Episcopal church in 1889 and a

The Three Mrs. Flaglers

Henry Flagler had three wives, and St. Augustine played a part in the story of his marriages. Flagler's first wife, Mary Harkness, the mother of his children, suffered from ill health. On a doctor's advice, the Flaglers traveled south to St. Augustine in 1876. Sadly, Mary died of consumption in 1881, but this visit inspired Flagler to invest a fortune in Florida hotels and railroads.

In 1883 Flagler married Ida Alice Shourds, a would-be actress who had been the Flagler children's nanny and Mary's caregiver. Ida traveled with Henry as he established more hotels and pushed the Florida East Coast Railway southward. In 1895 Ida Shourds Flagler was institutionalized for mental illness.

In 1901 the Florida legislature enacted a law allowing divorce on the grounds of incurable insanity. Flagler divorced Ida and married the vivacious Mary Lily Kenan that year. He was seventy-one and she was thirty-four. They moved into a new mansion in Palm Beach, but the couple returned to St. Augustine every Christmas to stay at his Ponce de Leon Hotel. When Flagler passed away in 1913 after a fall on his own marble staircase, Mary Flagler became one of the wealthiest women in the United States.

new Methodist church in 1891. He also paid for the construction of a YMCA building on Riberia and Valencia Streets in 1909, now the Flagler College Tennis Center.

Flagler also financed a large residence for black employees of his hotels. He acquired land along the Maria Sanchez River, filled it, and excavated the southern end of the creek to form the present Maria Sanchez Lake. On the landfill bordering existing Lincolnville, he built the Ponce de Leon Barracks. Located at the northwest corner of St. Francis and Cordova Streets, the building is now known as Lakeview Condominiums at St. Augustine. Its plain facade is deceptive. Each unit has a charming private deck off the back door and a view of the river.

The Ponce de Leon Barracks once housed African-Americans who worked in Flagler's hotels.

Flagler Beyond St. Augustine

Flagler soon expanded his vision for Florida from a winter Newport at St. Augustine to an American Riviera, with a string of resort towns down the east coast of Florida. After Flagler constructed a rail line to Palm Beach, he added two hotels and his magnificent private mansion, Whitehall, there.

The Over-the-Sea Railway

Between 1905 and 1912, Henry Flagler extended the Florida East Coast Railway to Key West, his crowning achievement. Key West was a large city by the standards of the day, with about twenty thousand residents. Located on a tiny island 128 miles from the Florida mainland, it couldn't be reached by land.

When the U.S. government announced plans in 1905 to construct the Panama Canal, Flagler realized that Key West would be the U.S. deepwater port closest to the canal. Furthermore, Key West was already a major coaling station with a naval base. A railroad link would allow coal to be shipped in by train.

The Florida Over-the-Sea Railway became known as the eighth wonder of the world. Taking seven years to finish, at its peak, construction required four thousand men. Three hurricanes and unique engineering challenges added cost and time. Flagler proudly rode the first passenger train into the city on January 22, 1912. The Labor Day Hurricane of 1935 destroyed parts of the line, shutting it down. The company sold the right-of-way to the state, and U.S. Highway 1 opened in 1938, using some of the same bridges.

SITES TO SEE

Confederate Memorials in the Plaza

Throughout the South, very few original Confederate memorials remain standing. Anna Dummett, the sister-in-law of General William J. Hardee, funded the one in the Plaza de la Constitución. Erected in 1872, the twenty-five-foot-high obelisk contains marble panels carved with the names of the St. Augustinians who fought for the Confederates, including Anna's nephew Willie J. Hardee. The names reflect the Spanish, Minorcan, and English heritage of the city and include old St. Augustine families like DuPont, Hurlburt,

The monument in the Plaza de la Constitución honors the men of St. Augustine who died in Confederate service.

Llambias, Papy, Hardee, and Ponce. The north and south faces of the obelisk display crosses, and concrete posts topped with cannonballs and linked with chains surround the monument.

Anna Dummett presided over the Ladies Memorial Association from its beginnings in 1866 until she died in 1899. In 1907 a St. Augustine chapter of the United Daughters of the Confederacy took the name the Anna Dummett Chapter.

Lighthouse/Lighthouse Museum

In 1824 builders erected the first lighthouse at St. Augustine near the site of a previous Spanish watchtower on ships' masts, located on the ocean shore of Anastasia Island. The first keeper, Minorcan John Andreau, died in 1859 after a fall from the tower, and his wife, Maria de los Dolores Mestre Andreau, then tended the light. It stayed in service until Paul Arnau, St. Augustine's pro-Confederate customs officer, hid the lens during the Civil War. After the war, local officials worried that beach erosion endangered the tower. A coquina breakwater only slowed the erosion so the government purchased a five-acre site half a mile inland, and workers began construction on a new lighthouse in 1871. Designed by Paul Pelz, later one of the architects of the Library of Congress in Washington, D.C., the new lighthouse began operation on October 15, 1874.

The new tower incorporated brick from Alabama, ironwork from Philadelphia, granite from Georgia, and a Fresnel lens imported from France. The lightkeepers stored kerosene for the lamp in a separate oil house. A duplex was completed in 1876, providing living quarters for the head keeper and two assistant keepers.

Although the keepers' house received electricity in 1925, the lighthouse continued to use oil until 1936. By 1971 an automated system completely replaced the need for lightkeepers. After a fire at the keepers' home in 1970, the Junior Service League restored the structure in 1980 and opened the present-day museum in 1988. You

This Victorian duplex, shaded by massive oak trees, housed the lighthouse keeper, his assistants, and their families.

can climb the tower and take in a magnificent view of St. Augustine, the surrounding county, and the ocean.

The Oldest Drugstore

An authentic old drugstore occupies a building that once served as a tavern and tobacco store. Built by Antonio Gomas in 1739, the building was moved to its present location on Orange Street in 1887 by pharmacist T.W. Speissegger. The Harris Foundation purchased the building in the 1980s and opened it as a free museum, supported by sales in the museum store.

Today the shop displays nineteenth- and early twentieth-century medicines and drugs behind glass cases. The store also maintains a large collection of modern herbal selections for sale in bulk from jars, ranging from addowart and catnip to yellowroot. An attached

You can find a fascinating collection of nineteenth-century herbal tonics, remedies, and spices inside the Oldest Drugstore.

ice cream shop at the east side of the building serves as the rallying point for the trolleys of Old City Tours. The Oldest Drugstore's prominent location near the visitors center, the City Gates, and the trolley tour line makes it a common stop for St. Augustine visitors.

Although builders of most of the eighteenth-century structures surviving in St. Augustine used masonry or coquina, the Oldest Drugstore remains one of very few constructed of wood. Despite its earlier construction and long history, its displays reflect the mid and late nineteenth century.

Markland House
Dr. Andrew Anderson first started building Markland House in 1839, the year he died in a yellow fever epidemic. His widow, Clarissa, expanded the building, located at 102 King Street. Their son, also named Andrew, served as Flagler's personal physician when Flagler stayed in St. Augustine. Andrew sold the property to the east of

Markland House to Flagler in 1887 for the Ponce de Leon Hotel, now Flagler College.

At the turn of the twentieth century, the younger Dr. Anderson dramatically altered Markland. He converted the simple, two-story home into an impressive mansion by adding a west wing, with a library and a dining room finished in Victorian panels, as well as a kitchen off the rear of the house. He expanded the second floor with additional bedrooms and replaced the square columns in front of the house with ornate, round Corinthian ones.

Anderson's heirs sold Markland House to Flagler College in 1968. It briefly served as the college president's house and then became a classroom building until the 1980s. Then the college converted the building to faculty and staff offices and used it for special functions. Flagler College arranges tours of the building, available on a limited basis.

Grace United Methodist Church

The original congregation of Grace United Methodist Church held their first services in the parlors of the Old Florida House Hotel. George Atkins of Asbury Park, New Jersey, organized the first St. Augustine Methodist Episcopal Church in 1881. The small congregation met in several locations until 1884, when the Reverend Samuel Payne raised money for the construction of the Olivet Methodist Episcopal Church. The church was planned to be built on the southwest corner of Cordova and King Streets, but Henry Flagler had already started construction of the Ponce de Leon Hotel across King Street, and he envisioned a central court surrounded by three hotels, which would require the Olivet Church property.

Flagler offered to build the Methodist congregation's church in exchange for a deed to the prized downtown location. John H. Carrère and Thomas Hastings, who also designed the Ponce de Leon and Alcazar Hotels, designed Grace United Methodist Church, located at the corner of Carerra and Cordova Streets. Workers began construction on the new church in 1886 and completed it the next year.

Formally opened with dedication services in January 1888, the church reflects the Spanish Renaissance Revival style. Grace United Methodist Church, Memorial Presbyterian Church (described in the next section), and Flagler's three hotels all represent the Moorish, Spanish, and Italianate Renaissance Revival styles. They created a unique ambience along the western side of St. Augustine's downtown area.

Memorial Presbyterian Church

Henry Flagler had the Presbyterian church built in 1889 and dedicated it in 1890 as a memorial to his daughter, Jennie Louise, who had recently died in childbirth. St. Mark's Basilica in Venice, Italy, provided the model for the design.

Inside, striking features and details reflected Flagler's desire for architectural and design effect. You can see the original lighting fixtures, pews, and an imported, hand-carved mahogany choir screen. The bronze chandeliers and twelve torchlike lights at the ends of the pews were converted from gas to electricity in the 1920s. Architects John Carrère and Thomas Hastings specified Italian marble floor tiles closely resembling those in the Venetian basilica. German artist Herman Schladermundt designed the ninety-two stained glass windows, which were installed in 1902. Thirteen of them contain quotations from the Apostle's Creed; a leaflet available at the entrance describes the location and symbolism of these windows.

The history room displays a model of Flagler's personal home, Kirkside. A family crypt at the church contains the remains of Henry Flagler; his first wife, Mary; his daughter, Jennie Louise; and his granddaughter, Marjorie.

The original church organ, installed in 1889 and rebuilt in 1927, served the church for eighty years. In 1969 the minister and church organist sought funding to replace the worn-out organ and installed the current one, built on the spot in 1970–71 by Boston firm Aeolian-Skinner. The organ has more than five thousand pipes, ranging from thirty-two feet to less than one foot tall.

Villa Girasol

Directly across from Memorial Presbyterian Church, at 35 Valencia Street, Villa Girasol often attracts the attention of passersby. Francis A. Hollingsworth, an architect hired by Flagler to work on the Florida East Coast Railway, built the home in 1905. Hollingsworth later had his own private architecture practice in the city in 1922. With its clay-tile roof, Villa Girasol is a fitting and unique part of the neighborhood but is not open for tourist visits.

Villa Girasol, across from Memorial Presbyterian Church, combined poured concrete with Mission Revival architecture.

These ruins of the school stand behind the St. Benedict the Moor Church.

St. Benedict Church and School

Set back from the street on Martin Luther King Avenue in Lincolnville stand the 1898 ruins of the St. Benedict the Moor School. First known as the St. Cecilia School, it is where the Sisters of St. Joseph taught. St. Katherine Drexel founded the school to serve the African-American community.

The St. Benedict the Moor School enrolled between ninety and one hundred pupils per year. It operated from 1898 to 1968, when the Catholic Church integrated its schools in St. Augustine.

In 1909 workers began building the Catholic church that stands in front of the school ruins. When the church opened in 1911, both school and church were renamed in honor of St. Benedict the Moor, patron saint of African-Americans. St. Benedict was an African-

Sicilian friar who lived from 1526 to 1589. Known as the Holy Negro, he was canonized in 1807. A St. Benedict Benevolent Society was formed among black Catholics in St. Augustine before the Civil War.

The church added the rectory next door in 1915. The Josephite Fathers of Baltimore pastored here for many years.

Villa Zorayda

Boston millionaire Franklin Smith built Villa Zorayda in 1883 as a winter home, pioneering the use of poured concrete mixed with crushed coquina. He ordered the building as a one-tenth–scale replica of one section of the Alhambra Palace in Granada, Spain. Smith drew the name Zorayda from Washington Irving's *Tales of the Alhambra*. Published in 1821, the book had initiated the fascination with Moorish culture and architecture in the United States. One of the book's stories, "Legend of Three Beautiful Princesses," tells of the sisters Zayda, Zorayda, and Zorahyda. The middle sister, Zorayda, "had a great feeling for beauty, which was the reason, no doubt, of her delighting to regard her own image in a mirror or a fountain, and of her fondness for flowers and jewels, and other tasteful ornaments." Smith, an avid collector of "tasteful ornaments," regarded Zorayda an appropriate name for his private castle in St. Augustine.

Villa Zorayda earned fame as one of the first structures in Florida in the Moorish Revival style, which incorporated minaret-like towers, circular windows, crenellated walls, and airy passageways. Other homes, hotels, and commercial structures in St. Augustine reflected some of the same motifs—found in Southern Spain and throughout the Ottoman Empire—as did motion-picture theaters and lavish hotels around the nation through the 1920s. St. Augustine contains some of the best preserved, surviving examples of the nineteenth-century beginnings of Moorish Revival architecture.

This statue of Henry Flagler welcomes you to Flagler College.

The Three Flagler Hotels

Henry Flagler operated three luxurious hotels in St. Augustine, all founded between 1887 and 1889. Today the grand structures dominate the intersection of King and Cordova Streets, just west of the plaza. Their Spanish Renaissance and Moorish Revival architecture is both impressive and extravagant.

In New York City, Flagler lined up young architects John Carrère and Thomas Hastings to design the first hotel. After this boost to their careers, Carrére and Hastings went on to many significant assignments, including the New York City Public Library on Fifth Avenue.

Flagler built the Ponce de Leon and Alcazar as a pair. He envisioned the Ponce as a formal hotel that would cater to the wealthiest clients. The Alcazar welcomed slightly less wealthy, informal guests. The Ponce served three meals a day, the Alcazar, only breakfast. Furthermore, the Ponce had a short winter season and then closed. Those who wished to stay longer moved to the Alcazar, which had a slightly longer season. The Alcazar included an arcade of shops, a casino, and a swimming pool.

In 1888 Flagler purchased the Casa Monica Hotel from Franklin Smith and renamed it the Cordova. In the same year, he opened the Ponce and Alcazar hotels. The casino and pool section of the Alcazar opened a year later. Unfortunately, the pool's water had a sulfuric smell not remedied until 1892, when the hotels began using water pumped in from the waterworks Flagler built in west St. Augustine. The sulfuric smell still hangs about artesian well–fed fountains such as the one in the front courtyard of Flagler College. Flagler's waterworks still stand at 254 West King Street.

By the late 1890s, hard times had hit the three grand hotels. The Great Depression ruined employment as well as investments, and tourism began to fall off. Tastes changed, and the Gilded Age values that had spawned the winter Newport concept were already dated by the first decade of the twentieth century. Flagler's own promotion of Palm Beach and, later, Miami, drew visitors farther south. As

---

Monica

Saint Monica was the mother of Saint Augustine. A devoted Christian, she was credited with converting Augustine to the faith, convincing him to be baptized at age thirty-three while he was residing in Italy. Monica is shown in one of the stained-glass windows in the Cathedral Basilica that document the life of Augustine, and Franklin Smith's Casa Monica Hotel is named for her.

visitors started to travel by automobile during and after World War I, they wanted the convenience of a motor court or motel. In 1923 the original three hotels still showed a profit, but after that they lost money.

Flagler Hotels: The Later Uses

Otto C. Lightner, publisher of *Hobbies* magazine, bought the Alcazar in 1947 to house his vast and eccentric personal collections, ranging from matchbooks to fine china. He tore down a bridge that connected the Alcazar and Cordova Hotels over Cordova Street, and he installed a wooden floor over the swimming pool. He housed his collections in rows of poorly labeled glass cabinets. The museum operated for only two years before Lightner died in 1950. The city managed the museum, but it fell into disrepair.

In 1973 the city of St. Augustine converted the Alcazar into a city hall and opened a newly designed Lightner Museum in part of the structure in 1974. The old casino has never been completely reused, but builders converted the pool area to a mall of small shops with a cafe at one end. From your table in the cafe, you can easily visualize the original indoor swimming pool.

The Ponce de Leon remained a hotel until 1967, when the newly organized Flagler College purchased it. You can tour some of the ornate college's rooms. The college has ten thousand square feet of historic space, including the rotunda room, where tours assemble. Louis Tiffany personally designed the stained-glass windows in the dining hall, resulting in the largest surviving private collection of Tiffany windows. Throughout both the interior and exterior of the structure, you'll see numerous architectural details, including the sculpted frogs and turtles in the front fountain, the ornate gargoyle-like downspouts, the Spanish Renaissance towers, and the spectacular domed ceiling in the entrance hall.

This perforated light sconce inside Casa Monica replicates the metalwork still practiced in Morocco.

In 1990 a group of entrepreneurs purchased the Cordova and elegantly restored and reopened it under its original name, the Casa Monica. Moorish Revival furnishings and fixtures fill the lobby and restaurant. Corbelled beams, pierced-metal light fixtures, and the Gold Room and Sultan's Room dining areas all capture the fanciful, imaginative vision of Franklin Smith from a bygone era.

Union Generals' House

Located at 20 Valencia Street, behind the college and between Memorial Presbyterian Church and Cordoba Street, is a home that has been converted into administrative offices by the college. The Union Generals' House derives its name from Union Generals John McAllister Schofield and Martin D. Hardin, who lived there in retirement. Hardin was one of the last surviving generals of the Civil War. He died in 1923 and is buried at the U.S. National Cemetery behind the St. Francis Barracks on Marine Street. His widow restored the Lady of La Leche Chapel at the Mission Nombre de Dios site in his honor. In the 1980s, when the college planned to tear down the Union Generals' House to construct a more modern office building, protests from history-minded St. Augustinians saved the building. A small model of the structure serves as a birdhouse in the front yard.

These mannequins represent a chain gang at the Old City Jail. The group sometimes causes passing motorists to do a double take.

Old City Jail

Built in the Victorian Queen Anne style of brick and stucco, this structure served as the city jail for more than sixty years. A tour of the jail highlights facilities for up to seventy-two prisoners, as well as living quarters for the county sheriff. The original cellblocks contained separate areas for men and women. Costumed interpreters play the role of deputies and show off a gallows as well as a large collection of guns used during crimes. Lifelike mannequins outside provide a photo opportunity, and a movable jail stands at the edge of the parking lot. The cagelike wagon transported prisoners to work details on highways.

Chapter 7

The Recent Century
1914–2013

Auto Tourism

Florida tourism saw a brief setback during World War I. However, by the 1920s, a new breed of automobile tourists began to arrive in Florida. The Dixie Highway, which connected Montreal to Miami through the Midwest in 1915, had an eastern segment, part of which followed U.S. Routes 1 and 5A just blocks west of downtown St. Augustine. Throughout Florida, facilities for automobile tourists proliferated. Trailer parks flourished on nearby Anastasia Island, where motorists from the North could enjoy the novelty of driving directly on the beach.

Dr. Andrew Anderson funded several monuments in an effort to introduce visitors to the city's unique heritage. Civic organizations continued his work by posting dozens of historical markers, preserving historic structures, and developing small, specialized museums.

Attractions during the 1920s and 1930s included the Alligator Farm on Anastasia Island and, farther south, Marineland, the nation's first dolphin research and entertainment facility. World War II saw much of the nation's tourist industry come to a grinding stop, with rationing of tires and gasoline, but St. Augustine continued to draw visitors. The sights of St. Augustine became a weekend pass destination for troops stationed at nearby military facilities, such as Camp Blanding, about seventy miles to the west, and Jacksonville Air Station, about the same distance to the north. The influx of soldiers, sailors, and airmen helped compensate for the drop-off of campers and motel tourists. These military men would spur post-war tourism when they later brought their new baby boom families to Florida.

After World War II, Floridians readily welcomed the less-affluent middle class tourist from the North, establishing new attractions that ranged from a carousel for children to Ripley's Odditorium, Potter's Wax Museum, and more sophisticated museums. Racial segregation in Florida, however, restricted the number of black tourists in the 1950s. That would begin to change in the 1960s.

Civil Rights Era

In 1954, in *Brown v. Topeka,* the Supreme Court declared unconstitutional the long-standing legal basis for the segregation of public schools, the "separate but equal" rule. Over the next decade, the Civil Rights movement sought to extend racial integration to colleges, parks, and beaches. The struggle changed shape in the early 1960s, as black leaders and local activists sought equal access to privately owned public facilities such as bus lines, restaurants, hotels, and theaters. Throughout the South, five-and-dimes such as Woolworth's willingly accepted black customers buying goods but denied them access to the low-cost lunch counters located in the same stores. Civil rights activists focused on this practice for reform early in the 1960s.

St. Augustine remained in the national spotlight over Civil Rights for several reasons. Although located in the Deep South, the city hardly seemed like a typical Southern town. Much of its revenue derived from Northern white visitors who came from cities and states with much less racial segregation than in the South. Northerners had never heard of most Southern towns of comparable size—St. Augustine's population remained under fifteen thousand in 1960—but St. Augustine had a national reputation as a place to visit. Furthermore, the city had an established black community, with families who proudly traced their ancestry in the city back to before the Civil War era.

The media attention brought national civil rights leaders, both black and white, to the city. These included the mother of the governor of Massachusetts, Mary Parkman Peabody, and black leaders Andrew Young, Ralph Abernathy, and Dr. Martin Luther King Jr.

Changing Tastes

Although the opening of Disney World in 1971 led to the demise of much of Florida's old roadside tourist attractions, St. Augustine survived the so-called Disneyfication of the state. Historical tourism was professionalized in the 1970s and was later led by local historians and curators. New attractions for wider audiences with more sophisticated and specialized interests took hold, with wine tasting, ale production, a chocolate factory, and about forty art galleries. Hands-on attractions designed to appeal to children supplemented the more traditional historical displays. Local disputes between preservationists and those who wanted more commercial development continued throughout the 1970s and 1980s.

By 2013 St. Augustine had become the premier tourist destination in northeast Florida, drawing an estimated two million visitors a year. Its many sites tell the story of the city's 450-year history and the 500-year history of Florida. The sites serve as three-dimensional documents of the military, social, and cultural history of the city.

SITES TO SEE

Dr. Anderson and His Memorials

While Anna Dummett emphasized St. Augustine's Confederate legacy, Dr. Anderson sought to move past Civil War antagonisms and highlight symbols that represented the city's Spanish heritage

Two lions, sculpted by Raffaello Romanelli, mark the Bridge of Lions, which emphasizes the city's connection with León, the birthplace of the Spanish discoverer of Florida, Ponce de León.

and its place in the United States. He sponsored the construction of the Ponce de León statue at the east end of the plaza, as well as the two sculpted lions that mark the entrance to the Bridge of Lions. On November 11, 1921, Dr. Anderson had the flagpole erected west of the plaza to commemorate World War I veterans and Armistice Day. The flagpole has a unique engraved, bronze base by sculptor Charles Adrian Pillars (1870–1937).

Dr. Andrew Anderson funded a flagpole as a memorial to St. Augustine citizens who fought in World War I. This ornate base was sculpted by Charles Pillars.

St. George Street

The city closed St. George Street to automobile traffic in 1990. The shopping venues here are housed in a wide range of historic structures, many from the eighteenth century.

Ripley Museum

Robert Ripley was once a guest at the Warden Castle Hotel, operated by writer Marjorie Kinnan Rawlings and her husband in the early 1940s. He decided the building would be an ideal place to house his collection of oddities, but although he offered to buy Warden Castle after World War II, the owners turned him down several times.

Robert Ripley was an avid collector of items from the Orient and traveled the world to find bizarre and unusual things and people. A

At Ripley's Believe It or Not Museum, this automobile, the smallest ever in regular production, greets you in the lobby.

talented artist, he created a newspaper cartoon called "Believe It or Not" and also hosted a radio program that featured reports on the oddities he found, including the tallest man (eight feet, eleven inches tall) and the shortest man (twenty-two inches tall). Fascinated with items such as shrunken heads, torture devices, vampires, animal mutations, and the smallest car (made on the Isle of Man in the Irish Sea), Ripley displayed many of these strange things in his odditoriums.

Following Ripley's death in 1949, his estate finally purchased Warden Castle and opened a museum. Ripley Entertainment, Incorporated, has since created thirty-one such odditoriums around the world. From Atlantic City to Copenhagen, London, and Malaya, the facilities draw hundreds of thousands of visitors annually.

St. Augustine's Warden Castle now contains a three-story odditorium that continues to fascinate visitors, especially children of

> **Ghost Tours**
>
> A number of ghost tours are available in St. Augustine: St. Augustine Hearse Tour; Paranormal Store and Tours of St. Augustine; Creepy Pub Crawl; Ghosts and Gravestones Trolley Tour; and Ghostly Experience Walking Tour.
>
> Most tours are led by costumed interpreters and include stops at Augustine's old cemeteries, as well as reportedly haunted sites such as the Old Jail and the lighthouse. Tours highlight accounts of ghost spotting, legends of past tragedies, and results of recent investigations into paranormal episodes. Most of the tours start around 7:00 or 8:00 P.M. and run for up to two hours.

a certain age who delight in the grotesque and peculiar. The Ripley company also runs a local trolley tour line.

Potter Wax Museum

George L. Potter always remembered a childhood visit to London, where he toured Madame Toussaud's Wax Museum, and he vowed to set up a similar attraction in the United States. He commissioned the Gems Studio in London to construct wax figures and had them shipped to St. Augustine between 1945 and 1946. Since the British wax sculptors had cast some of the figures in sitting positions, Potter actually had to buy seats on an airplane for them.

Potter demanded strict order, maintaining the museum with a long list of rules and regulations for the guides and detailed specifications for their uniforms. As the first wax museum in the United States, it became a regular St. Augustine attraction.

After Potter passed away in 1979, his family continued to operate the museum, but they lacked Potter's enthusiasm for the collection. Beginning in 1985, they auctioned off most of the collection. However, then-curator Dottie White stopped the auction

This 1927 merry-go-round landmark has provided fun for children in St. Augustine since 1994.

and moved the remainder of the collection to the corner of King and Aviles Streets in 1986. In 2013 the Potter Wax Museum moved to its new location at 31 Orange Street, immediately adjoining the Oldest Drugstore. It still displays more than 160 historical figures and celebrities from movies, television, music, and sports.

Carousel

A noted and well-established landmark, the St. Augustine Carousel is located at 180 San Marco Avenue in Davenport Park at the intersection of US 1 and San Carlos Avenue. It is a must-see for visitors with young children. A different, old-fashioned tune plays during each ride, reminiscent of the days of county fairs, carnivals, and visiting circuses.

    C.W. Parker built the carousel in 1927. Circus performer Gerard

Soules discovered it in a barn in Mystique, Michigan, and bought it for $25,000. For a while, the carousel operated in a zoo in Fort Wayne, Indiana. Gerard Soules' brother James inherited the carousel after Gerard's death in 1992. James restored it with help from Carl Theel of Theel Manufacturing and transported it to Davenport Park in 1994.

NEARBY ATTRACTIONS

Three nearby attractions represent the modern cultural and economic history of St. Augustine. The newer World Golf Hall of Fame attracts golf enthusiasts from around the country and the world. Other sites have longer histories, reflecting the continuing interest in local Florida wildlife that has drawn visitors since the days of William Bartram and John Audubon.

World Golf Hall of Fame

The World Golf Hall of Fame is located about fifteen miles northwest of St. Augustine just off I-95 in the World Golf Village. A worldwide consortium of twenty-six golf organizations sponsors the museum, which houses permanent and temporary exhibits. Permanent exhibits focus on the history of the game of golf, techniques, major players and organizations, golf course design, and dress and equipment.

A ten-minute video in the Championship Moments Theater provides a front-row seat for some of the most famous shots in golf, featuring such greats as Nancy Lopez, Arnold Palmer, and Jack Nicklaus. An exhibit features memorabilia of recent inductees into the Hall of Fame. The striking tower, visible from miles away, holds a collection of major championship trophies from the Players Championship, the Ryder Cup, and World Golf Championship matches. A golf simulator lets you try various famous courses, including St. Andrews, the Plantation Course at Kapalua, Hawaii,

The present-day Alligator Farm is a direct successor to the original established in 1893.

and the Firestone Country Club in Akron, Ohio.

You can test your skill outdoors as well on an eighteen-hole putting green. Another outdoor exhibit, the Challenge Hole, resembles the seventeenth hole at the Tournament Players Club at Sawgrass, Ponte Vedra, Florida. A prize print awaits you if you put two on the green, 132 yards over water.

Alligator Farm

The Alligator Farm has operated at its present location since 1923. The facility captures the spirit of early tourism in Florida and remains one of very few Florida attractions that have survived for more than a century under private ownership. The farm popularized interest in the alligator and contributed to the 'gator as Florida's state image.

The Alligator Farm has one of the world's largest collections of alligators in captivity. Feeding time is a major attraction.

George Reddington and Felix Fire founded the original South Beach Alligator Farm. The attraction flourished during World War I, adding thousands of reptiles and hundreds of alligators. After a fire, the owners purchased the present ten-acre tract on Anastasia Island. George bought out his partner in the early 1930s, and George and wife Nellie managed the Alligator Farm. In 1937 they sold the facility to W.I. Drysdale and F. Charles Usina, who successfully publicized the Alligator Farm nationally.

Drysdale and Usina built the stuccoed, mission-style entrance and gift shop complex that stand today. They worked assiduously to collect alligators and various wildlife specimens from other

Gomek

In 1997 the largest alligator in captivity died at the St. Augustine Alligator Farm. Gomek had lived at the farm since 1989 and was thought to be at least sixty years old. Captured in Papua, New Guinea, he was eighteen feet long and weighed about two thousand pounds. Today his preserved carcass is on display in a special tribute building at the farm, together with artifacts from New Guinea.

By hooking a harness to a line, you can fly directly over the alligators and other wildlife at the Alligator Farm.

attractions, including the North Miami Zoo, the Daytona Beach Alligator Farm, the Daytona Airport Zoo, and the Florida Museum of Natural History.

After World War II, the Alligator Farm, like other attractions that focused on wildlife, became much more sophisticated, combining educational and informational programs with simple entertainment.

Research conducted at the farm in the 1970s involved scientists from the University of Florida.

In March 2011, the Alligator Farm added an interactive activity called Crocodile Crossing. You can don a harness, clip to a safety line, and follow a rope walkway directly over the exhibits. The route involves an obstacle course with more than fifty "challenges" and has been dubbed "the first challenge course in the world over a zoo."

Marineland

Marineland, just south of the Matanzas Inlet on Highway A1A, began as Marine Studios in the late 1930s. Its founders included Cornelius Vanderbilt Whitney and W. Douglas Burden, both heirs to nineteenth-century shipping and railroad developer Cornelius Vanderbilt, as well as Count Ilia Tolstoy, grandson of Russian novelist Leo Tolstoy, and Sherman Pratt, who, like Henry Flagler and William Warden, was an early executive of Standard Oil. Whitney, Burden, Tolstoy, and Pratt planned a scientific research facility to house captured species of fish and marine mammals. The public was welcomed in order to provide funds for continuing research. The water tanks were designed with many portholes to allow visitors to view the sea life and to allow filmmakers to film motion pictures in the era before underwater cameras.

Marineland originated the term "oceanarium" to describe its unique seawater aquarium. On opening day on June 23, 1938, the facility squeezed in thirty thousand visitors; the traffic backed up on Highway A1A from both north and south, preventing thousands more from visiting. Marine Studios soon became the largest attraction in Florida. The combination of sound scientific research, entertainment, and educational value set the pattern for the success of later oceanariums elsewhere in the country.

During World War II, Marineland closed because of gas and tire rationing, and the government requisitioned much of the facility's equipment for war-related purposes. Norman Baskin, Marjorie Kinnan Rawlings's husband and former proprietor of the Warden Castle Hotel in St. Augustine, operated the Dolphin Restaurant and Penguin Bar at the facility. Until the opening of Disney World in 1971, Marineland continued to draw more visitors than any other attraction or facility in the state.

After a 2004 hurricane, the facility reopened in 2006 as the Marineland Dolphin Conservation Center. Once again, huge crowds attended. The present dolphin habitat offers hands-on experiences, including "touch-and-feed" sessions, swimming with dolphins, and extended sessions of assisting the professional dolphin trainers on staff.

GOURMET EXPERIENCES

Entrepreneurs know that modern tourists will frequent places that create a product that can be eaten or imbibed and offer a sophisticated place to sample it. A1A Ale Works, San Sebastian Winery, and the Chocolate Factory fit the bill. When so many foods and beverages come packaged in retail stores far removed from production, viewing the manufacturing and preparation process takes on a certain nostalgic charm.

A1A Ale Works

A1A Ale Works occupies space in the Plaza Building, built in 1888 and once home to the Surprise Store, which claimed to be "the leading department store on Florida's east coast." The building became the Plaza Hotel in 1934; from 1946 until 1986, it housed Potter's Wax Museum. Iron columns support the surrounding porch, decorated with elaborate ironwork reminiscent of New Orleans–style architecture.

The original Plaza Hotel had its entrance on Avenida Menéndez, facing the Matanzas River. Entering through the doorway, you see the ornate staircase to the second floor and, off the former lobby, passageways leading to an interior shopping mall housing a number of retailers, several eateries, and a Cuban cigar shop.

San Sebastian Winery

At this winery, located at 157 King Street and overlooking the San Sebastian River, you can learn details of the winemaking process by watching a short video and also receive a guided, one-hour walking tour of the eighteen-thousand-square-foot winemaking facility, including the Oak Barrel Room for aging cream sherry and port wines.

A wine expert hosts the tasting counter. A gift shop carries items such as glassware, cooking utensils, gourmet food products, wine gift baskets, and wine accessories. The Pirate's Treasure Chest gift basket contains three vintner red wines and chocolates. The Cellar Upstairs has a rooftop blues bar that offers views of St. Augustine, a selection of wine and appetizers, and live music on the weekends.

The Chocolate Factory

Located at 139 King Street, east of San Sebastian Winery, the Chocolate Factory gives guided tours of the working factory area. You'll learn details of the history of the factory and of chocolate in general.

After military service, Henry Whetstone returned to his hometown of St. Augustine, determined to go into a family business. He and his wife, Esther, started small in 1966, making chocolate fudge in their kitchen and selling it to tourists. They expanded their shop at 42 St. George Street, once the home of General Biassou (see

The Whetstone family now makes gourmet chocolates like these and offers guided tours of the factory.

Chapter 4). In 1984 they built a factory on Highway 312 outside of town that hosted popular tours and later opened the 139 King Street factory. They also have a shop on Anastasia Island at 13 Anastasia Boulevard.

Henry Whetstone's background as an engineer came in handy; he designed and made much of the machinery in the factory. Henry Whetstone or his son, Hank, personally made several of the machines described on the tour. Additionally, the Whetstones hold the patent on a chocolate metering pump. Whetstone once claimed

---

The St. Augustine Four

In July 1963, four sixteen-year-olds were arrested for trying to order hamburgers at the "whites only" lunch counter in Woolworth's. A local judge ordered them to promise that they wouldn't participate in any more demonstrations. When they refused, he jailed them and then sent them to reform school. National media reported the outrage. The four teenagers—Audrey Nell Edwards, JoeAnn Anderson Ulmer, Willie Carl Singleton, and Samuel White—missed Thanksgiving and Christmas with their families but were released by special order of the governor in January 1964.

Jackie Robinson praised the four for their courage. Robinson and his wife, Rachel, welcomed Audrey Edwards and JoeAnn Ulmer to their home in Connecticut to recover from their ordeal. They toured the 1964 New York World's Fair with Robinson.

The three surviving members of the St. Augustine Four and their families were honored at a 2004 celebration of their courage. The relatives of the fourth, the late Willie Singleton, also attended. Samuel White passed away in 2007. The St. Augustine Four are remembered among the heroes of the freedom movement.

---

that if you like mechanical things, such as automobiles, you would love the chocolate business.

For many years, Whetstone made chocolate for large companies such as Hershey and Mars. More recently, under the leadership of CEO Virginia Whetstone, daughter of the founders, the company specializes in artisan gourmet chocolates.

CIVIL RIGHTS SITES

The Northrup-Grumman Corporation has funded a series of markers throughout St. Augustine devoted to the "Freedom Trail," documenting many events of the Civil Rights struggle in the city. Sites include the home at 791 West King Street where Zora Neale

Rockford, Illinois, residents Gary and Tressa Anderson view this small monument in the plaza. The statue memorializes the 1960s' Civil Rights marches and demonstrations in St. Augustine.

Hurston rented a room in the early 1940s. There she completed her autobiography, *Dust Tracks on a Road*. The marker at her residence spells out these and other details of her life.

In 1960 Henry "Hank" Thomas, a native of St. Augustine, was a freshman at Howard University who tried unsuccessfully to get service at the lunch counter at McCrory's Five and Dime on St. George Street using the sit-in method. Today a historical marker inside the boutique mall at 158 St. George Street commemorates Hank's effort to assert his civil rights.

Another sit-in drew national attention in 1963. Police arrested four teenagers—Audrey Nell Edwards, JoeAnn Anderson Ulmer, Samuel White, and Willie Carl Singleton—for sitting at a lunch counter at the Woolworth's on King Street on July 18. They became

Local Civil Rights leader Dr. Robert Hayling lived in this two-story Victorian at 160 Martin Luther King Avenue. Ironically, the home had once been the residence of a pro-segregation judge.

known as the "St. Augustine Four," and their refusal to surrender their rights, as well as their imprisonment, focused nationwide news coverage on the Oldest City. A historic plaque at the tour bus stop in front of the former Woolworth's store on King Street facing the plaza details the event.

Several monuments in and around the plaza commemorate Andrew Young's speech in June 1964 and the march of blacks and whites to the plaza in support of equal rights. The city named the corner of St. George and King Streets "Andrew Young Corner." Inlaid panels in the park walkway there memorialize his remarks and those of President Lyndon Johnson. Erected in 2011, a small statue at the southeast corner of the plaza honors the "foot soldiers" of the Civil Rights Movement.

Dr. Martin Luther King Jr. stayed in the home of Janie Price prior to the Monson Motor Lodge swim-in.

In Lincolnville proper, reminders of the Civil Rights era abound. The Freedom Trail website lists all of the sites, many of which stand at readily visited spots, such as the Civil Rights House.

In 1964 the Civil Rights House became the residence of Dr. Robert B. Hayling, who emerged as one of the main organizers of Civil Rights activities in St. Augustine. A plaque displays a picture of Dr. Hayling, Dr. Martin Luther King Jr., and the Reverend Andrew Young meeting at the house.

The fact that visiting blacks stayed in private homes during this period didn't just reflect the hospitality of the local community. Black visitors simply couldn't get rooms at the town's hotels, motels, and motor lodges before 1964 since those venues were for whites only.

The Bell House hosted the protesters who participated in the swim-in at the Monson Motor Lodge.

The Reverend Martin Luther King Jr. stayed at the home of Janie Price at 156 Martin Luther King Avenue prior to participating in the demonstration at the Monson Motor Lodge on June 18, 1964. Janie Price had received nurses' training at Grady Hospital in the 1940s in Atlanta, where she had met students from Morehouse College, including Dr. King. Mrs. Price hosted both Dr. King and the Reverend Ralph Abernathy during their stays in St. Augustine.

Like Janie Price, another neighbor, Robert Victor Bell, a post office employee, and his wife, Willie Mae Bell, hosted visiting civil rights leaders, including J.T. Johnson, at their home at 112 Martin Luther King Avenue. A plaque explains that Johnson swam in the pool with others at the Monson Motor Lodge before the motel manager poured acid into the pool.

The St. Augustine Four, who led a sit-in at the downtown Woolworth's, attended Excelsior High School.

At the corner of Twine and Lovett Streets, a marker honors Henry and Kat Twine, who both marched in Civil Rights demonstrations. Henry served as president of the local NAACP and was also a city commissioner and vice mayor. Kat earned the city's de Aviles Award for her work in Civil Rights. When she died in 2002, city flags were lowered to half-staff.

A marker in front of a small black, one-story house at 177 Twine Street indicates the home of Lucille Plummer, a nurse and civil rights activist who hosted Mary Parkman Peabody, the mother of the governor of Massachusetts. Police arrested Mrs. Peabody for participating in a mixed-race sit-in at the Ponce de Leon Motor Lodge on March 31, 1964. Thugs attacked the small house in a firebombing attempt in 1965, but Mrs. Plummer remained active.

Kat Twine and the Freedom Hat

Mrs. Katherine (Kat) Twine (1925–2002) earned national fame as the "Rosa Parks of Florida." She was arrested so many times for her participation in non-violent protests that the local joke was, "What's harder to break than catgut?" Kat Twine.

At the peak of demonstrations in the summer of 1964, local police ran out of space in the jail for those arrested, so an outdoor stockade was set up under the blaring St. Augustine sun. To provide her own shade, Mrs. Twine wore a broad-brimmed hat whenever she thought she might be arrested. She proudly wrote "Freedom Now" on the hat and pinned on a large button from the 1963 march on Washington.

Mrs. Twine's "freedom hat" was seen in newspaper photographs across the nation whenever she was arrested at a demonstration. Later, when explaining the Civil Rights movement to school children too young to remember, she would show them the hat and they would draw pictures of her in her freedom hat. The hat has been preserved as perhaps the most famous relic of the St. Augustine Civil Rights movement.

The Plummer House was once firebombed when it hosted Mary Parkman Peabody, who came to St. Augustine to support Civil Rights demonstrations.

The Bethel Baptist Church at 222 Riberia Street hosted meetings of the NAACP Youth Council, advised by Dr. Robert Hayling and the Reverend Goldie Eubanks. They helped organize pickets and sit-ins at downtown lunch counters. The Reverend Andrew Young of the Southern Christian Leadership Council taught classes on the history of the Civil Rights movement in this church.

The oldest known slave cabin in St. Augustine still stands in Lincolnville. A marker at the corner of South and Blanco Streets stands next to the small structure. Now used as a garage for the main house on the corner, the building dates back to before the Civil War and was situated on the Buen Esperanza (Good Hope) Plantation.

The oldest surviving slave cabin in St. Augustine still stands at the corner of Blanco and South Streets in Lincolnville.

SOURCES

Here you'll find a listing of major published books and Internet sites that have proven useful to us as sources for Florida and St. Augustine history, from earliest times to the present. Several of the websites designed for visitors provide information about hours and access as well as historical information. Then, chapter by chapter, we list separate published works, both in print and on the Internet, that were useful, particularly with regard to the history of specific sites.

As we visited the historic sites, we gathered booklets, brochures, and fliers that are not widely available. Such sources are defined by historians as "fugitive materials." The brochures and fliers were free, and we recommend them to visitors seeking more information about individual sites. Most are published without a date, indicated here as n.d.

In addition, we made note of informative plaques mounted at the sites but have not listed them here. The vast majority of those historical plaques are accurate, and the information on them can be confirmed from other sources. Where discrepancies in minor details came up, we relied on the better-documented source.

The scholarly journal of the St. Augustine Historical Society, *El Escribano*, published numerous articles that have been reprinted as booklets or pamphlets. We also relied on several reprinted issues of the complete journal devoted to a single period or topic. As noted in the text, a number of issues of nineteenth-century periodicals and other contemporaneous documents provided direct quotes that shed light on an era.

However, the sites themselves are the most compelling documentation for this work and for the history of St. Augustine. Walking through the sites is a much more immediate way of experiencing the past. This method of interpreting historical sites as physical, three-dimensional documents of the past reflects the groundbreaking work *Nearby History: Exploring the Past Around*

You by David Kyvig and Myron Marty, originally published by the American Association for State and Local History in 1982 and updated in a second edition in 2000.

General Sources

Print

Adams, William R. *St. Augustine and St. Johns County: A Historical Guide.* Sarasota, FL: Pineapple Press, Inc., 2009.

Bolton, Herbert Eugene. *The Spanish Borderlands: A Chronicle of Old Florida and the Southwest.* New Haven, CT: Yale University Press, 1921.

Gannon, Michael, ed. *The New History of Florida.* Gainesville: University Press of Florida, 1996.

Graham, Thomas. *The Awakening of St. Augustine: The Anderson Family and the Oldest City: 1821–1924.* St. Augustine: The St. Augustine Historical Society, 1978.

Harvey, Karen. *America's First City: St. Augustine's Historic Neighborhoods.* St. Augustine: Tailored Tours, 1992.

Morison, Samuel Eliot. *The European Discovery of America: The Southern Voyages, 1492–1616.* New York: Oxford University Press, 1974.

Porter, Kenneth, ed. *The Black Seminoles: The History of a Freedom-Seeking People.* Gainesville: University Press of Florida, 1996.

Waterbury, Jean Parker, ed. *The Oldest City: St. Augustine, Saga of Survival.* St. Augustine: St. Augustine Historical Society, 1983.

Internet

City of St. Augustine. http://www.ci.st-augustine.fl.us/visitors/history_fullprint.html.

Nation's Oldest City. http://www.nationsoldestcity.com/.

Old City Web Services. http://www.oldcity.com/
    history-information.cfm.
Schafer, Daniel L. Florida History Online. http://www.unf.edu/
    floridahistoryonline/.
St. Augustine, Ponte Vedra, and the Beaches Visitors and
    Convention Bureau. http://beta.floridashistoriccoast.com/
    listings/history/sto313.
Wilson, Gil. "Dr. Bronson and Friends: A History of the
    City of St. Augustine." http://www.drbronsontours.com/
    bronsonhistorypage.html.

Chapter 1

Print

Archaeology at the Fountain of Youth Park: The Original St.
    Augustine. Trifold brochure available on-site, n.d. A project of
    the Historic St. Augustine Research Institute.
Juan Ponce de Leon: Additional Information. Single-page flyer,
    available on-site at the Fountain of Youth Park, n.d.
Mann, Charles C. *1491: New Revelations of the Americas before
    Columbus.* New York: Vintage, 2011.

Internet

Fountain of Youth. http://www.fountainofyouthflorida.com/history.
    php.
Historical archeology. http://www.flmnh.ufl.edu/histarch/fort_and_
    settlement.htm.
Mission Nombre de Dios. http://www.missionandshrine.org/.

Chapter 2

Print

Florida Park Service. Old Spanish Quarry, Anastasia State Park. Quadrifold brochure available on-site, n.d.

National Park Service. Self-Guided Walking Tour (Castillo de San Marcos). Quadrifold brochure available on-site, n.d.

Oldest House: The Gonzales-Alvarez House, A National Historic Landmark. Trifold brochure available on-site, 1983.

Suddeth, Frank. Colonial St. Augustine's Nine Wooden Forts. Trifold brochure available at Fort Matanzas National Park, 1981.

Internet

National Park Service, Castillo de San Marcos. http://www.nps.gov/casa/index.htm.

National Park Service, Matanzas. http://www.nps.gov/foma/historyculture/index.htm.

Chapters 3 and 4

Print

Curley, Michael J. *Church and State in the Spanish Floridas.* Washington, D.C.: The Catholic University of America Press, 1940.

The New Smyrna Colony: The Story of the First Greek Colony, A Mediterranean Odyssey to East Florida. Trifold brochure available on-site at the St. Photios Greek Orthodox National Shrine, n.d.

Panagopoulos, E.P. *New Smyrna: An Eighteenth-Century Greek Odyssey.* Brookline, MA: Holy Cross Orthodox Press, 1978.

Schafer, Daniel L. *William Bartram and the Ghost Plantations of British East Florida.* Gainesville: University Press of Florida, 2010.

Sisters of St. Joseph. The Father Miguel O'Reilly House Museum, 32 Aviles Street. Trifold brochure available on-site, n.d.

Sisters of St. Joseph. The Father Miguel O'Reilly House Museum Garden: Saint Augustine's Only Authentic Historic Garden. Trifold brochure available on-site, n.d.

Wright, J. Leitch, Jr. *British St. Augustine.* St. Augustine: Historic St. Augustine Preservation Board, 1975.

Internet

Genealogical research site on New Smyrna, Fr. O'Reilly, and Fr. Camps. http://halsema.org/people/theleonardifamily/culture/fatherpedrocamps/index.html.

Oldest Wooden Schoolhouse. http://www.oldestwoodenschoolhouse.com/VisitorInformation/index.htm.

Schafer, Daniel L. British Plantations and Farms on the St. Johns River, 1763–1784. http://www.unf.edu/floridahistoryonline/Projects/Plantations.html.

St. Photios shrine. http://www.st-augustine-travel-guide.com/greek-shrine.html.

The Tovar House. http://www.virtualtourist.com/travel/North_America/United_States_of_America/Florida/Saint_Augustine-764650/Off_the_Beaten_Path-Saint_Augustine-MISC-BR-1.html http://www.flheritage.com/preservation/markers/markers.cfm?ID=st.%20john.

Chapter 5

Print

Bulow Plantation Ruins Historic State Park. Bifold brochure available on-site, n.d.

Fretwell, Jacqueline T., ed. "Civil War Times in St. Augustine." *El Escribano,* vol. 23. Reprint of 1986 edition.

Griffin, Patricia C: "Mary Evans: A Woman of Substance. The Historical Basis for Eugenia Price's *Maria.*" *El Escribano*, vol. 14. Reprint of 1977 edition.

Historic Dunlawton Sugar Mill Gardens. Trifold brochure available on-site, n.d.

Joyce, Edward R. *St. Francis Barracks: A Contradiction of Terms.* St. Augustine: St. Augustine Historical Society, 1989.

Landers, Jane. "Africans and Native Americans on the Spanish Colonial Frontier." Chapter 3 in *Beyond Black and Red: African-Native Relations in Colonial Latin America* (Matthew Restall, ed.). Albuquerque: University of New Mexico Press, 2005.

Manucy, Albert. *The Houses of St. Augustine 1565–1821.* St. Augustine: St. Augustine Historical Society, 1962.

Neill, Wilfred T. *The Story of Florida's Seminole Indians.* St. Petersburg, FL: Great Outdoors Publishing Co., 1956.

Price, Eugenia: *Maria.* Nashville, TN: Turner Publishing Company, 1999. Reprint of 1977 edition. (The trifold brochure "In Search of Maria" available at the Oldest House Bookstore provides a walking tour describing the historical sites mentioned in the novel.)

St. Augustine Historical Society Research Library. Segui/Kirby Smith House Garden Guide. Trifold brochure available on-site, n.d.

St. Francis Inn. Single-sheet flyer available on-site, n.d.

Waterbury, Jean Parker. The Ximenez-Fatio House: Long Neglected, Now Restored (pamphlet). *El Escribano.* Reprint of 1985 edition.

Internet

Murat House and Dow Museum of Historic Houses. http://www. moas.org/dowmuseum.html.

Prince Witten. http://www.pbs.org/wgbh/aia/part2/2h56.html.

Segui/Kirby Smith House. http://st-augustine-historic-home.com/historic-st-augustine. htm.

Chapter 6

Print

Bowen, Beth Rogero. *St. Augustine in the Gilded Age.* Charleston, SC: Arcadia Publishing, 2008.

Graham, Thomas. Flagler's Grand Hotel Alcazar (pamphlet). *El Escribano,* Vol. 6. Reprint of 1969 edition.

Memorial Presbyterian Church. Trifold brochure available on-site, n.d.

Schafer, Daniel L. *Thunder on the River: The Civil War in Northeast Florida.* Gainesville: University Press of Florida, 2010.

Stained Glass Windows, Memorial Presbyterian Church. Trifold brochure available on-site, n.d.

Walch, Barbara. *Frank B. Butler: Lincolnville Businessman and Founder of St. Augustine, Florida's Historic Black Beach.* St. Augustine: Rudolph B. Hadley, 1992.

Waterbury, Jean Parker, ed. Henry M. Flagler, Florida's Foremost

Developer (pamphlet). *El Escribano,* Vol. 40. Reprint of 2003 edition.

Waterbury, Jean Parker. *Markland.* St. Augustine: St. Augustine Historical Society, 1989.

Chapter 7

Print

Lillios, Anna. *Crossing the Creek: The Literary Friendship of Zora Neale Hurston and Marjorie Kinnan Rawlings.* Gainesville, University Press of Florida, 2011.

Messenger, Cheryl, and Terran McGinnis. *Images of America: Marineland.* Charleston, SC: Arcadia Publishing, 2011.

Meyer, Edward. *Believe It or Not!* Orlando, FL: Ripley Entertainment, Inc., n.d.

Revels, Tracy. *Sunshine Paradise: A History of Florida Tourism.* Gainesville: University Press of Florida, 2010.

Rooney, Andy. *My War.* New York: Random House, 1996.

Smith, W. Stanford. *Camp Blanding: Florida Star in Peace and War.* Farquay-Varina, NC: Research Triangle Publishing, Inc. 1998.

Internet

Alligator Farm. http://www.alligatorfarm.us/history.html.

Fort Menendez. http://www.oldfloridamuseum.com/.

Lincolnville, Freedom Trail. http://www.accordfreedomtrail.org/.

Marineland. http://www.marineland.net/history.php.

Pirate and Treasure Museum. http://www.piratesoul.com/.

World Golf Hall of Fame. http://www.worldgolfhalloffame.

INDEX

Here are some other books from Pineapple Press on related topics. For a complete catalog, write to Pineapple Press, P.O. Box 3889, Sarasota, Florida 34230-3889, or call (800) 746-3275. Or visit our website at www.pineapplepress.com.

St. Augustine and St. Johns County: A Historical Guide by William R. Adams. A guide to the places and buildings where history can be found in America's oldest permanent settlement. Features color photographs throughout.

Flagler's St. Augustine Hotels by Thomas Graham. Describes Henry Flagler's three lavish hotels in St. Augustine. The Ponce de Leon, Flagler's preeminent hotel, now houses Flagler College. The Alcazar now holds City Hall and the Lightner Museum. The Casa Monica (previously called the Cordova) has been restored as a hotel. Full-color photographs.

Houses of St. Augustine by David Nolan. Photographs by Ken Barrett Jr.; watercolors by Jean Ellen Fitzpatrick. A comprehensive and fully illustrated book of the architecture of the Spanish, British, and American periods in the Ancient City. Full color.

Ghosts of St. Augustine by Dave Lapham. The unique history of St. Augustine has spawned more than 400 years' worth of ghosts. These 24 stories from the town's rich oral history offer a light yet sometimes hair-raising peek at the spooky side of the Oldest City.

Ancient City Hauntings: More Ghosts of St. Augustine by Dave Lapham. Enjoy 25 more scary stories from the author of *Ghosts of St. Augustine*. Visit the Oldest House, the Old Jail, Ripley's Believe It or Not Museum, the Oldest Schoolhouse, and many other haunted places that harbor spirits from ancient times.

Oldest Ghosts by Karen Harvey. Tales of unexplained exploits by the spirits dwelling in St. Augustine. Here are stories of spiritual contacts with no earthly justification, some funny, some sad, some frightening.

Historical Traveler's Guide to Florida, Second Edition, by Eliot Kleinberg. From Fort Pickens in the Panhandle to Fort Jefferson in the ocean 40 miles beyond Key West, historical travelers will find many adventures waiting for them in Florida. Eliot Kleinberg—whose vocation, avocation, and obsession is Florida history—has poked around the state looking for the most fascinating historic places to visit. In this second edition, he presents 74 of his favorites—17 of them are new to this edition, and the rest have been completely updated.

Time Traveler's Guide to Florida by Jack Powell. A unique guidebook that describes 70 places and reenactments in Florida where you can experience the past—and a few where you can time-travel into the future.

200 Quick Looks at Florida History by James Clark. Here are 200 short essays on Florida's 10,000 years of history, from the arrival of the first natives to the present. Packed with unusual and little-known facts and stories: The inventor of air conditioning died broke and forgotten; Florida printed $3 bills in the 1830s.

Historic Homes of Florida, Second Edition, by Laura Stewart and Susanne Hupp. Houses tell the human side of history. In this survey of restored residences, their stories are intertwined with those of their owners in a domestic history of Florida. Most of these houses are museums now; others are restaurants or bed-and-breakfasts. This new edition is updated and illustrated with color photographs.

Florida's Finest Inns and Bed & Breakfasts, Second Edition, by Bruce Hunt. From warm and cozy bed-and-breakfasts to elegant and historic hotels, this is the definitive guide to Florida's most quaint, romantic, and often eclectic lodgings. With photos and charming pen-and-ink drawings by the author.

Visiting Small-Town Florida, Third Edition, by Bruce Hunt. From Carrabelle to Bokeelia, Two Egg to Fernandina, these out-of-the-way but fascinating destinations are well worth a side trip or weekend excursion.

Best Backroads of Florida by Douglas Waitley. Each volume in this series offers several well-planned day trips through some of Florida's least-known towns and well-traveled byways. You will glimpse a gentler Florida and learn a lot about its history. Volume 1: *The Heartland* (south of Jacksonville to north of Tampa); Volume 2: *Coasts, Glades, and Groves* (south Florida); Volume 3: *Beaches and Hills* (north and northwest Florida).

Florida History from the Highways by Douglas Waitley. Journey along Florida's major highways and learn all of the roadside history on the way. Begins with a brief history of Florida.

Florida's Museums and Cultural Attractions, Second Edition, by Doris Bardon and Murray D. Laurie. This newly updated guide has a destination to suit every interest. You'll find more than 350 museums and attractions to choose from.